DAILY MEDITATIONS WITH THE HOLY SPIRIT

"You will receive power when the Holy Spirit comes upon you, and then you will be my witnesses." (Acts 1:8).

DAILY MEDITATIONS WITH THE HOLY SPIRIT

MINUTE MEDITATIONS FOR EVERY DAY CONTAINING A SCRIPTURE READING, A REFLECTION, AND A PRAYER

By
REV. JUDE WINKLER, OFM Conv.

Illustrated

CATHOLIC BOOK PUBLISHING CORP.
New Jersey

CONTENTS

IMPRIMI POTEST: Michael Kolodziej, OFM Conv.
Minister Provincial of St. Anthony of Padua Province (USA)

NIHIL OBSTAT: Rev. Msgr. James M. Cafone, M.A., S.T.D.
Censor Librorum

IMPRIMATUR: ✠ John J. Myers, J.C.D., D.D.
Archbishop of Newark

The Nihil Obstat and Imprimatur are official declarations that a book or a pamphlet is free of doctrinal or moral error. No implication is contained therein that those who have granted the Nihil Obstat and Imprimatur agree with the contents, opinions or statements expressed.

(T-582)

ISBN 978-1-958237-19-9

Printed in Korea 23 NT 1
catholicbookpublishing.com

INTRODUCTION

Come Holy Ghost, Creator Blest,
And in our hearts take up thy rest.
Come with thy grace, and heavenly aid,
To fill the hearts which thou hast made,
To fill the hearts which thou hast made!

ANYONE who has ever taught a Confirmation preparation class has been struck by how difficult it is to explain who the Holy Spirit is. We can say what the Holy Spirit does (sanctifies, fills us with His gifts, guides us and the Church) and we can speak of symbols used for the Spirit (the dove, fire, oil, water, wind, breath, etc.). But Who is the Holy Spirit?

We have even changed the Spirit's name within many of our lifetimes. We used to call the Spirit the "Holy Ghost," but now we say the "Holy Spirit." The reason for the change is that languages often change the meanings of particular words. While "Ghost" might have been a perfectly good word to use decades ago, it no longer is because it implies a phantasm more than a spiritual entity.

One of the most difficult things is to explain how the Holy Spirit could be a person. It is easier to think of the Spirit as a force or a way that God makes Himself known to us. Yet we know that the Holy Spirit is the third person of the Blessed Trinity. Maybe we just have to accept that this is a mystery, and we can never fully understand Who the Spirit is.

But that doesn't mean that we cannot form a relationship with the Spirit. The Holy Spirit has been breathed into our hearts at creation and again when Jesus rose from the dead. The Spirit, the love of God, fills us and empowers us. The Spirit, in fact, loves us more than we could ever love ourselves.

This meditation book presents a short passage from Sacred Scripture dealing with the Spirit or the Spirit's gifts. There is an explanation of that verse and a short prayer to apply the fruits of our meditation to our everyday lives. May this meditation book serve you well as you reach out to the Spirit, our friend and our love.

Father Jude Winkler, OFM Conv.

N the beginning God created the heavens and the earth . . . and a mighty wind swept over the waters. —Gen 1:1-2

JAN. 1

REFLECTION. The phrase translated here as "mighty wind" could also be translated as "the Holy Spirit."

When we live in sin, the Spirit is a mighty wind that shakes the foundations of our lives. When we live in God's love, the Spirit broods over our hearts to bring forth life.

As we make our New Year's resolutions, we are called to choose life and love.

PRAYER. *God, please fill my heart with Your Spirit so that my life will be filled with meaning and peace.*

UT as for me, I am filled with the power of the Spirit of the Lord, with authority and with might. —Mic 3:8a

JAN. 2

REFLECTION. Micah the prophet realized that he was speaking in God's name. He would never have dared speak upon his own authority. He felt that God's Spirit empowered him to prophesy. Therefore, he could boldly confront even kings and generals.

How do I know when I am saying what God wants me to say?

PRAYER. *Spirit of God, fill me with Your word and Your confidence.*

O prophecy ever came from human initiative. Rather, when people spoke as messengers of God, they did so under the inspiration of the Holy Spirit. —2 Pet 1:21

JAN. 3

REFLECTION. This text speaks of the fact that the Holy Spirit inspired prophecy as well as the other writings of the Bible. "Inspired" literally means that the Spirit breathed into these authors so that what they said and wrote were God-filled words.

That same Spirit inspires us as we read and study Sacred Scripture.

PRAYER. *Word of God, may You inspire my mind and my heart.*

N wisdom there is a *beneficial* spirit that is also humane, steadfast, secure, free from anxiety and all powerful . . . —Wis 7:23

JAN. 4

REFLECTION. The Spirit of God teaches us how we can live our faith with great generosity of spirit.

There is a vertical dimension to our faith (praising and worshiping God), but there is also a horizontal dimension to our faith in which we show our love to our sisters and brothers, God's beloved children.

PRAYER. *God, may I praise You even as I serve Your children.*

HE fullness of wisdom is *fear of the Lord,* she is present with the faithful in the womb. —Sir 1:14

JAN. 5

REFLECTION. Fear of the Lord does not mean to be afraid of God. It means to stand in awe and wonder before the greatness of the Lord.

When we recognize that God is God and we are creatures, we develop a healthy sense of humility. We acknowledge our need for wisdom and grace, which are both gifts of the Holy Spirit.

PRAYER. *Give me Your wisdom and grace, Lord, so that I may be filled with awe and wonder.*

ISDOM is a refulgence of eternal light, a spotless mirror of how God works. —Wis 7:26

JAN. 6

REFLECTION. Wisdom reveals the radiance of God's glory to us, and thus helps us to recognize that there is another level of reality beyond what we can see and perceive with our mortal eyes.

Like the Magi who followed the star of Bethlehem, we seek the source of this radiance.

PRAYER. *Spirit of wisdom, guide me with the light of Your revelation.*

WILL ask the Father, and He will give you another Advocate [Paraclete] to be with you forever, the Spirit of Truth . . .

—Jn 14:16

JAN. 7

REFLECTION. The word Paraclete has many meanings. It could be translated as advocate or counselor or consoler or vindicator, etc. All of these meanings are intended.

Jesus was the first Paraclete. When Jesus ascended to the Father, They sent the Holy Spirit upon us to be all these things for us.

PRAYER. *Holy Spirit, be my advocate, my counselor, my consoler, and my vindicator.*

S Susanna was being led out to her execution, God stirred up the holy spirit of a young man named Daniel . . .

—Dan 13:45

JAN. 8

REFLECTION. The Holy Spirit reveals many things to us. In addition to the sublime truths of our faith, the Spirit helps us figure out right from wrong.

The Spirit comes to our assistance when we suffer for the good choices that we have made (e.g. being misunderstood, mocked, etc.)

PRAYER. *Spirit of God, give me the courage to give witness to the truth and to defend the weak and powerless.*

HE fruit of the Spirit is love, *joy*, peace, patience, kindness, generosity, faithfulness, gentleness and self-control.

—Gal 5:22-23

JAN. 9

REFLECTION. Even though the Disciples suffered persecution, they were filled with joy. One would have expected them to be depressed or angry or resentful. The very fact that they responded to persecution with joy is a sign that the Spirit was guiding their actions.

We can use that same test with our own words and actions.

PRAYER. *Fill me with joy, O Spirit of God, even when things are not going all that well.*

UCH hope will not be doomed to disappointment, because the love of God has been poured into our hearts through the Holy Spirit . . .

—Rom 5:5

JAN. 10

REFLECTION. The Holy Spirit is the love between the Father and the Son and Their love for us.

When we receive that Spirit, we learn the true meaning of love and service. This also fills us with hope, for the consolation we receive is a type of guarantee that God will fulfill all of His promises to us.

PRAYER. *Teach me the true meaning of love, O Lord.*

HE saved us through the bath of rebirth and renewal by the Holy Spirit Whom He lavished on us abundantly through Jesus Christ our Savior. **—Tit 3:5-6**

JAN. 11

REFLECTION. Human beings were created when God breathed His Spirit into Adam. We were renewed when Jesus breathed His Spirit into His Disciples.

This breath is renewed in each of our hearts when we turn back to the Lord and reject what might drag us down.

PRAYER. *Breathe Your Spirit into my heart, O Lord.*

ALONG both banks of the river, there were fruit trees of every kind; their leaves would never fade, nor would their fruit fall. **—Ezek 47:12**

JAN. 12

REFLECTION. Ezekiel speaks of the grace that would flow out of the temple. This grace is a gift of the Holy Spirit Who lifts up our prayers to the Lord and Who shares God's love with us.

We experience that same grace when we celebrate the Eucharist.

PRAYER. *Spirit of God, may our hearts and our land be filled with Your life.*

O this the Spirit bears witness, for the Spirit is truth . . .

—1 Jn 5:6

JAN. 13

REFLECTION. How do we know that what we believe is true? One of the most important ways is to listen to the Holy Spirit speaking in our hearts.

We can sense that what we are hearing makes sense. That feeling is coming from the Spirit Who is assuring us at the deepest core of our being that we have found the truth.

PRAYER. *Teach me Your truth, O Spirit of God, so that I may always walk in it.*

INNOW not in every wind, and do not start off in every direction.

—Sir 5:11

JAN. 14

REFLECTION. It is essential to discern what the Spirit wants when we are making important choices in our lives.

Through prayer, fasting, spiritual reading, spiritual advice, discernment of signs, sorting out our hidden motivations, etc., we develop a sense of what God wants of us.

PRAYER. *Guide me in Your ways, O Lord, so that I may know what You want me to do.*

THE prayer of a righteous man is powerful and effective.

—Jas 5:16

JAN. 15

REFLECTION. Prayers are God-filled words in which our love and God's love are joined. That love embraces the people for whom we are praying, and love always changes people and situations.

This doesn't mean that we will always get what we want, but Jesus does promise that we will get what we need.

PRAYER. *Lord, teach me how to pray.*

WHO has ever known Your counsel except You had given wisdom and sent Your Holy Spirit from on high? —Wis 9:17

JAN. 16

REFLECTION. When we try to discern God's will, we are asking the Holy Spirit to clarify what course of action we should take. In this sense, we are surrendering to that which the Spirit wants of us.

Does that surrender mean that we are losing our freedom, or are we actually more free when we choose to embrace God's will?

PRAYER. *Not my will, but Your will be done, O Lord.*

ILLED with the Holy Spirit, Jesus returned from the Jordan and was led by the Spirit into the desert for forty days . . .

—Lk 4:1-2

JAN. 17

REFLECTION. The Spirit led both Jesus and St. Anthony the Hermit into the desert to help them purify their motives so that they might dedicate themselves totally to the will of the Father.

At times, we must pull back and let the Spirit help us to purify our intentions.

PRAYER. *Lead me into the desert, O Spirit of God, so that I may purify the motives of my heart.*

N wisdom, there is a spirit . . . which is *all seeing* and which penetrates all spirits . . .

—Wis 7:22-23

JAN. 18

REFLECTION. Sometimes when we do things that we should not be doing, we pretend that God cannot see us, and He therefore does not know what we are doing.

But God knows everything. God even knows our hidden motivations, for the Spirit of God knows us better than we know ourselves.

PRAYER. *Spirit of wisdom, reveal that which is hidden, clarify that which is confused.*

THEY rebelled and grieved His Holy Spirit, so He turned against them like an enemy and fought them.

—Isa 63:10

JAN. 19

REFLECTION. When we sin, God doesn't hate us. The Holy Spirit, the Spirit of love and compassion, is always offering God's love to us.

When we sin, we are turning our backs on that love. We have made ourselves enemies of the One Who always loves us.

PRAYER. *May I turn back to You, O God, so that I may love You as much as You love me.*

DO NOT grieve the Holy Spirit of God Who has marked you with His seal for the day of redemption.

—Eph 4:30

JAN. 20

REFLECTION. When we were sealed by the gift of the Spirit, God showered His incredible dignity upon us. We are invited into the very life of the Holy Trinity.

To turn away from that life of grace, to sin, would be a disastrous rejection of what God has called us to be.

PRAYER. *Lord, help me to be what You created me to be.*

OD has called us to holiness, not to impurity. Anyone who rejects these instructions rejects . . . God Who also gives His Holy Spirit to you.

—1 Thes 4:7-8

JAN. 21

REFLECTION. God places the Holy Spirit within our hearts. Like the Eucharist which is bread that is so Spirit-filled that it becomes the body of Christ, so also our human bodies have become so Spirit-filled that we have become part of the Mystical Body of Christ.

We must treat our bodies with dignity and not allow them to be misused by practicing impurity.

PRAYER. *May I proclaim the Good News through the purity of my ways.*

RETHREN, we direct you to select from among you seven men of good reputation, men filled with the Spirit and with wisdom . . . —Acts 6:3

JAN. 22

REFLECTION. The first prerequisite for service in the Church is that the person be filled with the Holy Spirit.

Whether to minister or not is not really our own personal choice. It is the Spirit Who calls us to ministry and the Spirit Who gives us the courage and love to respond to that call with generosity.

PRAYER. *Teach me, Spirit of God, how I can serve Your holy Church.*

N these last days God has spoken to us through His Son . . . through Whom He created the universe . . . —Heb 1:2

JAN. 23

REFLECTION. It is through the Holy Spirit that God made Jesus present in the world. It was through that same Spirit that God spoke the Word that created the world (and that Word was Jesus).

This reminds us of how the Spirit re-creates the world to make it God's kingdom and how that same Spirit sanctifies our hearts.

PRAYER. *May your Spirit re-create me in Your image, O Lord.*

HEN they approached the border of Mysia, they tried to go into Bithynia, but since the Spirit of Jesus did not allow them to do so . . . —Acts 16:7

JAN. 24

REFLECTION. Bithynia had already been catechized by missionaries from Jerusalem, and Paul felt called to preach where the Word had never been preached.

The Spirit often guides us by strong attractions toward and strong feelings against a certain course of action.

PRAYER. *May I always listen to the promptings of the Spirit within my heart.*

NANIAS went forth and entered the house. He laid his hands on Saul and said . . . "regain your sight and be filled with the Holy Spirit."

—Acts 9:17

JAN. 25

REFLECTION. When Paul experienced the love of God in Christ and the gift of the Holy Spirit, his life was transformed. He no longer lived to do things. His life was centered on loving Someone.

Can I say that about myself? Is my faith a question of "doing" or of "loving"?

PRAYER. *May I never get so caught up with doing things that I lose sight of my true goal: love!*

O you, Timothy, my child, I am giving these instructions in accordance with those prophecies once made about you . . . —1 Tim 1:18

JAN. 26

REFLECTION. People in St. Timothy's community discerned that he was being called to a special ministry within the community.

This should have given him confidence, for Timothy had not made the decision himself. If the Spirit called him, then it would be the same Spirit Who would empower him with authority and courage.

PRAYER. *Holy Spirit, give me the gifts that I need to do Your work.*

I ASK that from the riches of His glory He may grant through His Spirit that you may be strengthened with power in your inner being. —Eph 3:16

JAN. 27

REFLECTION. True strength is not found in being stubborn or arrogant. It is found in allowing the Holy Spirit to dwell in one's heart so that one might be open to the Spirit's promptings.

It is that Spirit Who frees us from our selfishness for the Spirit reminds us that God is supposed to be the center of who we are and what we do.

PRAYER. *Enrich me with Your Spirit, O Lord, so that I may surrender to Your will.*

THUS I send my teaching forth like the dawn so that it might be made known in distant lands. —Sir 24:30

JAN. 28

REFLECTION. It is the Holy Spirit Who bestows the gifts of understanding and knowledge and wisdom. St. Thomas Aquinas so powerfully exhibited these gifts in his studies and his writings.

We pray to that Spirit to guide us in our own studies (whether they are formal studies or faith-filled prayer and reflection).

PRAYER. *May I always want to know more about my faith, Lord, so that I may be one with You.*

O I will heal them of their defection. I will love them freely, for My wrath is turned away from them.

—Hos 14:5

JAN. 29

REFLECTION. We are all sinners. We have all turned away from the Lord, but the Lord is always ready to take us back. When we sin we hurt ourselves, we break our own hearts.

The Father sends His Holy Spirit into our hearts to bring us forgiveness and to heal whatever damage we have done to ourselves.

PRAYER. *May Your Spirit of forgiveness bring healing to my heart.*

O! I will pour My Spirit upon you, I will acquaint you with My words.

—Prov 1:23

JAN. 30

REFLECTION. The Word of God is inspired by the Holy Spirit. The Spirit breathed holiness into the thoughts and talents of the sacred authors so that they produced much more than human words. They produced the very Word of God.

When we read Sacred Scripture in the Spirit, we encounter that living Word in all its power.

PRAYER. *May the Word of God speak to my heart and guide my ways.*

THUS I pour out instruction like prophecy and bestow it upon generations to come. —Sir 24:31

JAN. 31

REFLECTION. St. John Bosco, filled with the Holy Spirit's zeal, dedicated himself to the education of the young. He realized that the gift had been given to be shared with the next generation so that they might be guided in their development and led into God's ways.

What do I do to share my faith with others?

PRAYER. *Fill me with zeal, Holy Spirit, so that I may share my faith through word and deed.*

MOSES said, "Would that all the people of the Lord might be prophets! Would that the Lord might give His Spirit to them all!" —Num 11:29

FEB. 1

REFLECTION. When Moses chose the 72 elders of Israel so that he might share his authority with them, two of them received that gift in the camp. Rather than object to this, Moses spoke of how he wished that all would receive that gift.

Do I rejoice when others receive gifts from the Holy Spirit as much as I do when I receive those gifts?

PRAYER. *Holy Spirit, descend upon all Your people and share Your many gifts with them.*

ROMPTED by the Spirit, Simeon came into the temple. —Lk 2:27

FEB. 2

REFLECTION. Simeon, a man open to the workings of the Spirit, was able both to listen to God's promptings and to recognize the fulfillment of God's promise in the person of Jesus.

The Holy Spirit prepares us to hear God's call, and then that same Spirit helps us to recognize when the time is right to answer that call.

PRAYER. *Open my ears, Lord, to Your call and my heart to Your love.*

ESUS said, "Amen, amen, I say to you, no one can enter the kingdom of God unless he is born of water and the Spirit." —Jn 3:5

FEB. 3

REFLECTION. Jesus speaks of two things being necessary to enter the kingdom of God.

One must be born of water which means to receive the sacrament of Baptism so that one might make a public commitment to Christ. One must also be born of the Spirit to be renewed in one's heart by the breath of God.

PRAYER. *May my commitment to You, Lord, be seen in both what I do and who I am.*

E has poured wisdom forth upon all of His works, upon every living thing according to His bounty. He lavished her upon His friends. —Sir 1:8

FEB. 4

REFLECTION. God is not stingy with His gifts and His love. He pours them forth in abundance.

When we do good deeds, our hearts become more receptive to that love. When we sin, our hearts shut out the gifts that God is offering us.

PRAYER. *Lord, may I be as generous in my response to You as You are in granting me Your gifts.*

HIS is how we can be certain that we abide in Him and that He abides in us; He has given us a share in His Spirit. —1 Jn 4:13

FEB. 5

REFLECTION. Jesus came into this world so that we might live in communion with Him. That is why we were created in the first place.

It is the Holy Spirit Who is the union between the Father and Jesus and Who unites us with Them in a bond of eternal love.

PRAYER. *Holy Spirit, abide in my heart so that I may live and love in You.*

OU in turn became imitators of us . . . for despite great suffering you received the word with joy in the Holy Spirit.
—1 Thes 1:6

FEB. 6

REFLECTION. Joy is not necessarily happiness. Happiness is momentary gratification. One is not happy when one suffers, but one can be joyful.

Joy is the sense that we are where we should be. It is the firm belief that we are one with God no matter what is happening.

PRAYER. *Grant me Your joy, O Lord, and let me share it with those who have become discouraged.*

UR competence comes from God Who has empowered us to be the ministers of a new covenant, not written but of the Spirit. **—2 Cor 3:5-6**

FEB. 7

REFLECTION. St. Paul contrasts external observance of the rules with an interior conversion of love in the Spirit.

External actions might look good, but they really don't renew us. It is only when we fall in love with God, when God's love (the Holy Spirit) and our love become one that we become a new creation.

PRAYER. *Write Your new covenant upon my heart, O Lord, so that I may live fully in You.*

N wisdom there is a *keen* spirit that is unhampered, beneficent, kind and firm . . . —Wis 7:22-23

FEB. 8

REFLECTION. The Spirit of God is not like a dull knife that refuses to cut. The Spirit is like a sharp blade that can cut right to the heart of the matter.

The Spirit can help us to explore what is hidden and confused and to sort out our motivations so that we may be and do what is Spirit-filled.

PRAYER. *Spirit of God, send Your Word, Your sharp two-edged sword, into my heart as You did to the Blessed Virgin Mary.*

ESUS, filled with the power of the Spirit, returned to Galilee . . . —Lk 4:14

FEB. 9

REFLECTION. Jesus, being obedient to the will of the Father, always followed the direction of the Spirit. This is also what the Church is supposed to do and exactly what it does in the Acts of the Apostles.

Jesus' obedience is the model for what each of us should do in our faith life.

PRAYER. *Guide me, Holy Spirit, into God's ways.*

NYONE who knows God will listen to us . . . This is how we can distinguish the spirit of truth from the spirit of falsehood. —1 Jn 4:6

FEB. 10

REFLECTION. It can be difficult to sort out the truth from lies. We have to listen to the Spirit speaking in our hearts, but we also have to listen to the voice of the Magisterium.

In this letter, the elder reminds the community that he has been given authority by the Holy Spirit to help guide it in the ways of the Lord.

PRAYER. *Lord, protect those whom You have chosen to lead the Church.*

ISDOM is resplendent and unfading, and she can readily be perceived by all those who love her. —Wis 6:12

FEB. 11

REFLECTION. It is difficult to describe God for He is so far beyond our understanding. We must therefore use words like "light" and "resplendence."

The Spirit lights up our ways and shines forth gloriously. The Spirit is so glorious that He draws us to Himself and fills us with a sense of wonder.

PRAYER. *Lord, let me see Your radiance, if only for a second.*

N the Lord's day, I was caught up in the Spirit and I heard behind me a loud voice. —Rev 1:10

FEB. 12

REFLECTION. On the Lord's day, Sunday, the visionary was open to the Holy Spirit in a special way. Because his heart was open, he was able to hear what the Lord was saying to him.

Christ's voice came through as powerful as if it were a blowing trumpet. If we are not open, then no matter how loud Christ's voice is, we will not be able to hear it.

PRAYER. *Speak to me loud and clear, O Lord, so that I may know Your will.*

HE Spirit Himself intercedes for us with sighs that cannot be put into words. —Rom 8:26b

FEB. 13

REFLECTION. There are times when words are not enough. We don't even know how to phrase what we need for we are not even sure what it is that we most need.

At times like that, the Spirit must pray for us, lifting up our unknown needs to the Father in the name of Jesus.

PRAYER. *Loving Spirit of God, please pray for me when I'm not able to pray for myself.*

E has appointed me to be a minister to the Gentiles . . . in order that they might become an acceptable offering consecrated by the Holy Spirit. —Rom 15:16

FEB. 14

REFLECTION. St. Paul speaks of his priestly service of presenting the Gentiles as a fragrant offering to the Father. Rather than being consumed by fire, this offering was sanctified by the fire of the Holy Spirit.

We, too, are called to be God's co-workers in bringing people to salvation.

PRAYER. *Lord, may I always be willing to share my faith with those who need to hear the Good News.*

HOSE who are led by the Spirit of God are children of God.

—Rom 8:14

FEB. 15

REFLECTION. What does it mean to be a "child of God?" Parents love their children and want what is best for them. There is an intimacy in their relationship that survives both time and struggles.

Children must trust and obey their parents and learn life's lessons from them. Parents should be willing to die for their children, and it breaks their hearts when they see their children making bad mistakes.

PRAYER. *Our Father, Who art in heaven . . .*

ALVATION was the subject of intense scrutiny and investigation by the Prophets . . . —1 Pet 1:10

FEB. 16

REFLECTION. The Prophets thought that they were speaking about their own times, but the Holy Spirit often had another level of meaning for what they said.

The Spirit encouraged them to speak in a way that also referred to God's plan for us, a plan to save us from our sins and to invite us to share in God's glory for all eternity.

PRAYER. *Lord, help me to recognize that there is more going on than I can readily perceive.*

HE wind blows where it chooses, and you hear the sound of it, but you do not know where it comes from or where it goes. —Jn 3:8

FEB. 17

REFLECTION. In Biblical languages, the word for "Spirit" is the same as the word for "wind." Jesus was telling Nicodemus that we cannot control the action of the Holy Spirit.

The Spirit often surprises us in ways that we would never have expected, sometimes moving peacefully and other times forcefully.

PRAYER. *Surprise me, Spirit of God. May I always be open to Your promptings wherever they may lead me.*

RACE to you and peace from . . . the seven spirits before his throne . . .

—Rev 1:4

FEB. 18

REFLECTION. The Book of Revelation speaks of the Spirits standing before the throne of the Father.

Seven is the perfect number. The Spirit is manifested to us in many, many different ways. We encounter the Spirit in life, and love, and revelation, and forgiveness, and compassion, etc.

PRAYER. *May I encounter Your grace in so many ways today, Holy Spirit, and may I live in that grace.*

OW He was referring here to the Spirit . . . (Who) had not yet been bestowed because Jesus had not yet been glorified.

—Jn 7:39

FEB. 19

REFLECTION. To receive glory is to live in the fullness of God's love, a love that carries Jesus to the Cross, Resurrection, and Ascension.

Why could the Holy Spirit not descend before this happened? Maybe because Jesus had to make explicit on the Cross how profound His love was so that the Spirit's love could be understood.

PRAYER. *Give me Your gift of the Holy Spirit, O Lord, so that I may be willing to carry my cross each day of my life.*

THE Most High possesses all knowledge and sees things that are to come from of old. —Sir 42:18b

FEB. 20

REFLECTION. All throughout Sacred Scripture we hear that God has a plan for us.

When we discern that plan and embrace it, we find a profound sense of peace. When we reject that plan because we think it asks too much from us, we find a sense of uneasiness and frustration.

PRAYER. *Spirit of God, teach me to surrender to Your plan.*

A SPIRITUAL person discerns all things, and he is himself subject to no one else's judgment. —1 Cor 2:15

FEB. 21

REFLECTION. If we live in the Spirit, we will be able to see into the hearts of those around us.

Of course, if we see that their hearts are broken because of life or even because of their own sins, we will experience compassion for them and desire their healing.

PRAYER. *Spirit of God, help me to see myself and others as You see us.*

PASSING into holy souls from age to age, wisdom produces friends of God and Prophets. —Wis 7:27b

FEB. 22

REFLECTION. As the Holy Spirit passes into our hearts, we become friends of God. The Spirit calls us to share that relationship with others.

This is our prophetic call: we are sent out to proclaim the Good News that God loves us so much that He would call His Son to die on the Cross out of love for us.

PRAYER. *May I always glory in the wisdom of the Cross and give witness to that wisdom in my everyday life.*

WHOEVER has ears should listen to what the Spirit says to the Churches. Anyone who is victorious shall not be harmed by the second death. —Rev 2:11

FEB. 23

REFLECTION. St. Polycarp was not afraid to die for the faith. The Spirit had assured him that life awaited him and not death.

It is the Spirit who gives us the courage to die to ourselves in order to live with Him.

PRAYER. *Spirit of God, may I always remember that death is not the end but rather is a new beginning.*

ONE and the same Spirit works all of these things, distributing them individually to each person as He wills.

—1 Cor 12:11

FEB. 24

REFLECTION. St. Paul spoke of the fact that the Holy Spirit is the source of all spiritual gifts (also called charisms).

The Spirit gives those gifts to whomever the Spirit wishes (so we should not complain that we don't have this or that gift). Nevertheless, we can pray to be given a particular gift if that is the Spirit's will.

PRAYER. *Give me the gifts, Holy Spirit, that I most need, and teach me to long for those gifts that are most useful.*

THE angel said to me, "These words are trustworthy and true, for the Lord God Who inspires the Prophets has sent His angel . . ."

—Rev 22:6

FEB. 25

REFLECTION. The same Holy Spirit Who inspired the Prophets also inspired the author of the Book of Revelation.

This book was not written to predict the end of the world, but rather to tell us what we should do while we await the Day of the Lord: we should give witness to the Good News.

PRAYER. *Lord, together with the Holy Spirit I call out, "Come, Lord Jesus."*

WILL come down and speak with you here. I will take some of the Spirit that is upon you and bestow it on them. —Num 11:17

FEB. 26

REFLECTION. Moses was not jealous of his authority. He wanted to share it with the elders in the camp. He realized that the grace of the Spirit of God was not intended to be hoarded.

The same is true for us. We should want to share our talents with those who need them most.

PRAYER. *May I always be willing, O Spirit of God, to share my gifts with others.*

SPIRIT of *counsel* and of strength, of knowledge and fear of the Lord. —Isa 11:2

FEB. 27

REFLECTION. We frequently need other people's help to figure out what God wants of us. It is relatively easy to sort out what is bad from what is good, but it is much more difficult to sort out what is good from what is better and what is bad from what is worse.

The Holy Spirit gives us the counsel we need through external and internal signs of grace.

PRAYER. *May I never be afraid to seek advice from You, O Holy Spirit, and from those whom You have sent into my life.*

ND the prayer of faith will save the sick person, and the Lord will raise him up. —Jas 5:15

FEB. 28

REFLECTION. A faith-filled prayer is an expression of love for and trust in God. The Spirit of God raises this love up to the Father and communicates the Father's love to us.

Sometimes this brings physical healing. Sometimes this brings healing of one's spirit (finding peace even if one is not healed physically).

PRAYER. *Teach me to trust in the power of prayer, O Lord.*

T is the decision of the Holy Spirit and also our decision not to lay any further burden upon you . . . —Acts 15:28

FEB. 29

REFLECTION. In the early days of the Church, the Apostles recognized that the Holy Spirit was guiding them.

That Spirit still guides the Magisterium of the Church. The Pope is infallible when he speaks *ex cathedra* on faith and morals. The Spirit guides the decisions of Church councils. We are not on our own.

PRAYER. *Spirit of God, may I listen to Your voice when You speak through the Magisterium of the Church.*

HEN the Spirit of the Lord rushes upon you, Saul, you will join them in their prophetic state . . .

—1 Sam 10:6

MAR. 1

REFLECTION. When we are baptized, the Spirit gives us a new birth as children of God. Like King Saul, we are given the role of king and prophet.

As king, we have the authority to help guide society, the Church, and our family in God's ways. As prophet, we are called to look upon things through the eyes of God.

PRAYER. *Help me to know, Spirit of God, what it means to share in Christ's role as king, prophet and priest.*

[

ETER and John] laid hands on them and they received the Holy Spirit.

—Acts 8:17

MAR. 2

REFLECTION. When one lays hands on another, one's hands are stretched out so that they almost appear to be in the form of the wings of a dove.

Just as the Holy Spirit hovered over the waters and the Holy Spirit descended upon Jesus in the Jordan and upon the Blessed Virgin Mary and the Apostles on Pentecost Sunday, so the Spirit descends upon those over whom we pray.

PRAYER. *Lay Your hands on me, O Lord, and consecrate me in Your love.*

N wisdom there is a *kindly* spirit which is firm, secure and tranquil . . .

—Wis 7:23

MAR. 3

REFLECTION. If we live in the Spirit, we will want what is best for others. We will be creative in finding ways to support and encourage them.

When we wake up in the morning, one of our first thoughts should be how we can help others. When we speak about them, we should be sure that what we say is true, kind and helpful.

PRAYER. *Grant me a kindly spirit, Lord, so that I may reflect Your compassion for others.*

HE first man, Adam, became a living being; the last Adam has become a life-giving spirit. **—1 Cor 15:45**

MAR. 4

REFLECTION. The first Adam chose to sin, and when he did, he broke our hearts, damaging something precious inside of us.

The second Adam, Jesus, healed us of the wounds caused by that first sin. He breathed the Spirit back into us, filling us with so much life that even death could no longer conquer us.

PRAYER. *Fill me with Your life-giving spirit, Jesus, so that I may live with You forever.*

E plumbs the depths and He penetrates the heart; He understands their inmost being. —Sir 42:18a

MAR. 5

REFLECTION. There is no part of our lives that is unknown to God. No motivation with which the Spirit is not familiar. In fact, the Holy Spirit knows us better than we know ourselves for at times we can fool ourselves concerning what is really going on inside of us.

When we live in the Spirit, those hidden recesses of our heart are illumined.

PRAYER. *Spirit of God, light up the secret thoughts of my heart and the hidden desires of my soul.*

URNING in front of the throne were seven flaming lamps, the seven spirits of God. —Rev 4:5

MAR. 6

REFLECTION. In Scripture, one often finds the Holy Spirit spoken of in terms of fire. In this passage, we hear of flaming lamps, in other places tongues of fire, lampstands that burn the sacred oil provided by the two olive trees, a purifying fire, etc.

Fire produces light, heat burns away what is dead and promotes new growth.

PRAYER. *Consuming Fire, burn away the impurities of my heart.*

THE Word of God is living and active . . . It judges the thoughts and the intentions of the heart. —Heb 4:12a, c

MAR. 7

REFLECTION. We have often seen the effect words can have. A kind word can make someone's day. A criticism can shake one's confidence. A word of rejection can break a heart.

The Word of God is so much more powerful. It can transform civilizations, and yet be intimate enough to speak to the most secret recesses of our hearts.

PRAYER. *Speak to me, O Word of God, and recreate me in God's image and likeness.*

"COULD we ever find anyone else like him," Pharaoh asked his officials, "a man so filled with the Spirit of God." —Gen 41:38

MAR. 8

REFLECTION. Even Pharaoh, a pagan, could recognize the profound spirit of Joseph. Likewise, St. John of God was known as a profoundly spiritual, holy man.

When we allow the Spirit to reign in our hearts, people can sense it and they seek the peace that we have found.

PRAYER. *May I be so filled with Your Spirit, O God, that even strangers can sense Your presence in me.*

E are not debtors to the flesh and obliged to live according to the flesh. —Rom 8:12

MAR. 9

REFLECTION. Living according to the flesh means living a lifestyle that is worldly and materialistic. It does not bring us joy or peace. It only produces emptiness within our hearts.

If, however, we live a spiritual life, choosing what is good and holy and generous, we will live a life that is so profound, that even if we die, we will live forever.

PRAYER. *Spirit of God, teach me to die to myself to live in You.*

ISDOM that comes from above is first of all pure, then peaceable, gentle, and considerate, full of mercy and good fruits . . .

—Jas 3:17

MAR. 10

REFLECTION. How do we know whether we really possess the spirit of wisdom or whether we are simply being arrogant and think that we have all the answers?

This list of virtues serves as an examination of conscience to make sure that what we are sharing is not our own agenda or our pet peeves.

PRAYER. *Fill me with the virtues of wisdom, O Lord, so that I might overflow with Your grace.*

LL of them were filled with the Holy Spirit and began to speak in different languages, as the Spirit enabled them to do so. —Acts 2:4

MAR. 11

REFLECTION. When the people in the city of Babel built a tower to reach to the heavens, God confused their languages as a punishment for their arrogance.

When the Holy Spirit descended upon the Apostles on Pentecost, they were able to speak different languages. The confusion that divided people from each other was healed by the Holy Spirit.

PRAYER. *May my every word, my every thought, be Spirit-filled.*

CARCE do we understand the things upon earth, . . . but who could know the things of heaven? —Wis 9:16

MAR. 12

REFLECTION. Our human intelligence is limited. We study and research, but there is so much we don't know. How much of a chance do we have to understand the great mysteries of God?

And yet the Holy Spirit gives us insight into spiritual things, inviting us into an intimate relationship with God.

PRAYER. *Reveal Your secrets to me, O Spirit of God, and fill me with Your wisdom.*

ISDOM teaches us moderation and prudence, justice and fortitude. There is nothing in life more useful than these. —Wis 8:7b

MAR. 13

REFLECTION. The Spirit calls us to live virtuous lives. True virtue, though, as St. Augustine taught, lies in the middle, in prudence and moderation.

When we exaggerate one virtue over all the others, it can actually become a vice. What we are doing is really a form of perfectionism and spiritual pride.

PRAYER. *Lord, may I never allow my spiritual choices to become a form of spiritual pride.*

OD did not give us a spirit of timidity but rather a spirit of power and of love and of wisdom. —2 Tim 1:7

MAR. 14

REFLECTION. We sometimes think that the most Christian attitude is to keep quiet and avoid judgment of what others are doing. The temptation is to keep the peace at all cost.

There are times when we have to speak out in order to be faithful to what the Spirit calls us to be (as long as what we say or do is motivated by the true good of the other person).

PRAYER. *Teach me when to speak out, Spirit of God, and when to keep silent.*

HERE are different varieties of gifts, but the same Spirit.

—1 Cor 12:4

MAR. 15

REFLECTION. Each of us has received some charisms (gifts from the Spirit). These charisms might be found in our natural talents (to study, athletics, etc.). Others are more spiritual gifts (e.g. able to pray well, able to share one's faith with confidence, etc.). Some of these gifts appear to be everyday, almost mundane; other gifts are more spectacular.

Which gifts has God given to me?

PRAYER. *Spirit of God, shower Your gifts of grace upon me.*

ETER was astonished that the gift of the Holy Spirit should have been poured out on the Gentiles also.

—Acts 10:45

MAR. 16

REFLECTION. Peter knew what it meant to be anointed by the Spirit, so he could recognize when it occurred to others. Rather than be annoyed because they received the gift without his intervention, he was thrilled that God had worked in such a surprising way.

The Spirit often calls us to look beyond our sometimes myopic viewpoints and see what God sees in others.

PRAYER. *May I never reject those, O Lord, whom You have chosen in Your love.*

AM longing to see you so that I may bestow on you some spiritual gift to strengthen you, or rather, so that we may be mutually encouraged . . . —Rom 1:11-12

MAR. 17

REFLECTION. While Paul wanted to strengthen the faith of the Romans, he recognized that this community was also anointed by the Holy Spirit. They therefore had received gifts that he did not have, and Paul could learn something from them.

No one has a monopoly on the gifts of the Holy Spirit.

PRAYER. *Holy Spirit, may I always be ready to share Your gifts with others and receive Your gifts from them.*

OU will be able to perceive my understanding of the mystery of Christ. . . . [which] has been revealed to His holy Apostles and Prophets by the Spirit. —Eph 3:4-5

MAR. 18

REFLECTION. The ways of the Lord are not always easy to understand. This is why we need the revelation of the Spirit (in our hearts and through the Magisterium) in order to perceive what God wants of us.

On our own, we can never hope to figure it all out.

PRAYER. *Open my mind to Your revelation, O Spirit of truth, so that I may embrace the mystery of Your love.*

JOSEPH, son of David, be not afraid to receive Mary into your house . . . for this child has been conceived in her womb through the Holy Spirit. —Mt 1:20

MAR. 19

REFLECTION. St. Joseph trusted God's revelation although he could not fully understand the meaning of what he was being told. He responded to this call with great generosity of spirit, caring for Mary and her child.

His humble obedience to God's call and his generous compassion to Mary and Jesus give us an example of faith which was both profound and practical.

PRAYER. *St. Joseph, may I be as generous in my response to God's call as you were.*

IN wisdom there is a *tranquil* spirit that is all-powerful and all-seeing. —Wis 7:23

MAR. 20

REFLECTION. The Holy Spirit is a spirit of peace. If there are divisions in our community (or even within our own hearts), we have to ask whether these are due to the action of God's Spirit or if they are being instigated by evil spirits who celebrate division and judgmentalism.

Do my spiritual insights bring peace or discord to the community?

PRAYER. *Lord, grant me a peaceful spirit that calms and heals the wounds of this world.*

OD is the one who has prepared us for this destiny, and He has given us the Spirit as a pledge of this.

—2 Cor 5:5

MAR. 21

REFLECTION. We have been predestined to be saved. Even before we were created, God had written our names in the Book of Life.

God wants us to live in His love forever, but love can never be forced. So He courts us lovingly in the Holy Spirit as a foretaste of the glory to come.

PRAYER. *God, may I always live up to the destiny that You have in store for me.*

HE Holy Spirit of discipline flees away from deceit and withdraws away from senseless counsels. —Wis 1:5

MAR. 22

REFLECTION. We cannot hope to be truly spiritual people if we do not practice the spiritual disciplines. Prayer, fasting, study, confession, guidance, etc. help us to purify our intentions and actions so that we can live in the Spirit and not by our passions.

By practicing discipline in our spiritual life, we are able to distinguish true wisdom from foolishness.

PRAYER. *Lord, may my life of penance and other spiritual disciplines free my heart so that I may love You more.*

OD'S creative work continues effectively without ceasing upon the surface of the world. —Sir 38:8

MAR. 23

REFLECTION. If we look at creation, we can see God's fingerprints. It all reflects God's glory.

This is especially true when we gaze upon the never-ending vitality of nature. It's as if we are facing something new and wonderful every time we look at the world.

PRAYER. Creator God, may I always recognize the action of Your Spirit recreating this world in Your image and splendor.

AM speaking the truth in Christ . . . as my conscience bears witness for me through the Holy Spirit that I have great sorrow . . . —Rom 9:1-2

MAR. 24

REFLECTION. St. Paul says that it breaks his heart that the Jewish people haven't come to Jesus. He goes on to say that if his going to hell would mean that they would go to heaven, then so be it.

It is only in the Holy Spirit that one would make such an outrageously loving offer.

PRAYER. May my love for others be so profound that I would gladly give up what I consider to be most precious to me for their spiritual good.

THE Angel answered, "The Holy Spirit will come upon you, and the power of the Most High will overshadow you." —Lk 1:35

MAR. 25

REFLECTION. Jesus entered our world through the generous availability of Mary and the action of the Holy Spirit. Luke describes the scene in terms which recall the cloud that overshadowed the Tent of Meeting when God appeared to the people of Israel.

Mary was the new Ark of the Covenant, the vessel through which God appeared to His people.

PRAYER. *Hail Mary, full of grace . . .*

YOU did not receive a spirit of slavery leading to fear; rather, you received a spirit of adoption enabling us to cry out, "*Abba,* Father!" —Rom 8:15

MAR. 26

REFLECTION. God never intended for us to be robots that blindly follow His will. We were created to share in His glory. He breathed His Spirit into us so that we might share in His life. He sent His Son to die out of love for us.

He loves us more than any parent could ever love a beloved child.

PRAYER. *Spirit of God, remind me always that God is my Abba.*

F prudence renders service, then there is no better craftsman in the world than she.

—Wis 8:6

MAR. 27

REFLECTION. Wisdom does not lead us to extremes. The spirit of wisdom guides us in moderation and prudence. This does not mean that we shouldn't give our all, but we should try to do it in a way that is balanced.

A magnesium flame burns brightly but also burns away quickly. A regular flame might not give quite as much light, but it lasts much, much longer.

PRAYER. *Teach me Your prudence, O Holy Spirit, so that my faith may be constant and long lasting.*

HE Spirit of the Lord fills the whole world. The Spirit is all embracing and knows whatever people say.

—Wis 1:7

MAR. 28

REFLECTION. We cannot really say that God's Spirit is here or there. God's Spirit is everywhere, interpenetrating every dimension of all that exists.

There is nothing hidden from the Spirit of God, nothing that does not draw its life and existence from the Spirit's bounty.

PRAYER. *All-embracing Spirit of God, fill me and the whole world with Your love and wisdom.*

RETHREN, if anyone is detected committing a transgression, you who are spiritual must set him right in a spirit of gentleness. —Gal 6:1

MAR. 29

REFLECTION. Being filled with the Spirit does not make us feel superior to others. If anything, the more we are one with the Spirit, the more we should feel compassion for those who are living in sin. Like the Spirit, we should want them to be made whole in the love of God.

We therefore pray for them and lovingly invite them to change their ways.

PRAYER. *May I be an instrument of the healing and forgiveness of the Holy Spirit.*

ROM that day on, the Lord's Spirit rushed upon David. —1 Sam 16:13

MAR. 30

REFLECTION. God had chosen David to be the king of Israel as the successor of King Saul. God looked into David's heart and saw that it was pure.

But David could not rule God's people on his own. He needed wisdom and prudence and counsel from the Holy Spirit to be what God had invited him to be.

PRAYER. *Gracious Spirit of God, grant me those gifts which I need to fulfill the tasks that You have assigned to me.*

N wisdom there is an *agile* spirit that is clear, unstained and certain.

—Wis 7:22

MAR. 31

REFLECTION. While the Holy Spirit is an anchor of stability in our lives, the Spirit also challenges us to transform our lives in God's grace. We can easily get into a rut, and we need the Spirit's promptings to remind us that our faith is a journey.

Jesus said that the foxes have their lairs and the birds have their nests, but the Son of Man has no place to lay His head.

PRAYER. *God, teach me to be flexible when that is appropriate, and stable when that is what You want.*

HE Prophets have become wind for the word is not in them.

—Jer 5:13

APR. 1

REFLECTION. Many people claim to have had spiritual experiences and then later it is proven that this was not the case. Some are lying, others honestly believe that what they were saying is true while it was only a product of their desires.

What does the Church look for to determine whether an apparition is authentic?

PRAYER. *May I never chase after what is spiritually spectacular. May I always follow the guidance of the Church.*

LESSED are the poor in spirit, for theirs is the kingdom of heaven.

—Mt 5:3

APR. 2

REFLECTION. St. Francis of Paola and his followers sought to live lives of great humility. They did not allow their spiritual growth to make them arrogant.

I should often ask myself whether I feel superior to others because my spiritual life appears to be more profound than theirs.

PRAYER. *May I be a humble person, glorying only in what the Lord has done through me.*

OD, Who knows the heart, bore witness by giving to them the Holy Spirit just as He did to us.

—Acts 15:8

APR. 3

REFLECTION. In the writings of St. Luke, what is most important is that one's heart be open to God's will.

Ultimately, this is what is essential: that one be an honest seeker of the truth. The Holy Spirit is always ready to visit and inspire this type of person.

PRAYER. *Holy Spirit, pour out Your gifts into my heart as well of those of my family and friends.*

I HAVE filled him with a holy spirit of skill and understanding and the knowledge in every craft. —Ex 31:3

APR. 4

REFLECTION. Isidore was the father of encyclopedias, one of the first to arrange information in a highly organized manner. This is why he is the patron of computers.

He reminds us that we should not be myopic in our studies and interests, but rather expand our horizons to embrace as much of God's wonder as we can.

PRAYER. *Spirit of Wisdom, may I be as curious and filled with as much wonder as a child exploring the world for the first time.*

FULLNESS of wisdom is found in the fear of the Lord; she *inebriates* people with her fruits. —Sir 1:14

APR. 5

REFLECTION. We usually think of inebriation as something bad. When we are drunk, we are out of control and do things that we normally would not. But one can also be drunk with joy, with the Spirit, with enthusiasm.

Being out of control in these things and letting the Spirit take charge is really a good thing.

PRAYER. *Overwhelm me, Spirit of God, with the abundance of Your grace.*

[GOD has] given us the Spirit in our hearts, as a down payment of what is to come. —2 Cor 1:22

APR. 6

REFLECTION. God's seal is a sign of ownership. We belong to God for He has claimed us as His own.

The Spirit already dwells in our hearts as a sign that He has made His abode in us, and this communion is only the beginning of what God intends for us when all that keeps us from being one with Him is finally healed.

PRAYER. *Dwell in my heart, Holy Spirit, and make me Your own.*

THE Spirit of the Lord came upon me and He instructed me to say, "Thus says the Lord . . ." —Ezek 11:5

APR. 7

REFLECTION. The Prophet Ezekiel received a more ecstatic version of the gift of the Spirit than did many of his fellow Prophets. Some have wondered whether he might have been mentally ill.

Yet even if that is true, God worked through him for God does not choose those who are perfect but rather the broken.

PRAYER. *Holy Spirit, may I not see my brokenness as a curse but rather as an opportunity to grow in Your love.*

THEY made their hearts as hard as a diamond so as not to listen to the teachings that the Lord of hosts had sent by His Spirit. —Zec 7:12

APR. 8

REFLECTION. The Holy Spirit is always willing to teach us the ways of the Lord, but we can easily close our hearts to that instruction. This can be done consciously, or it can even be done in slow motion by simply not making the Spirit a part of our lives.

Laziness and indifference can be just as bad as rejection.

PRAYER. *May I never close off my heart to Your call, O Spirit, either by rejection or indifference.*

FOR when people . . . have shared in the Holy Spirit and . . . have fallen away, it is impossible to restore them to repentance. —Heb 6:4, 6

APR. 9

REFLECTION. If we have experienced the gift of the Spirit, how could we turn away? Some in the early Church thought that there was no possibility of forgiveness, but the Church eventually realized that God was willing to forgive every offense.

Are there any sins, in fact, that cannot be forgiven?

PRAYER. *Lead me to conversion, O Spirit of God, and forgive me my sins.*

O they remained in a prophetic state . . . but there was no sound, no one answered, and no one was listening.

—1 Ki 18:29

APR. 10

REFLECTION. In the early days of the Old Testament, many Israelites believed that Yahweh was their God but that other gods existed. This passage uses a triple negative to teach that the others gods are the "nothing-est," that Yahweh is the only God Who exists.

Do I have other gods in my life (work, pleasure, prestige, etc.)?

PRAYER. *Holy Spirit, may You continuously remind me never to allow other things to take the place of God in my heart.*

O the one who is victorious . . . I will give him a white stone . . .

—Rev 2:17b

APR. 11

REFLECTION. The white amulet represents a way of voting for one's candidate in the ancient world.

When we choose God with our lives and our love, God chooses us and calls us His beloved. The Spirit, the love of God, allows us to experience this even now.

PRAYER. *Choose me, O Lord, as Your own, and may I always choose You without reserve.*

ND they were all filled with the Holy Spirit and proclaimed the word of God fearlessly. —Acts 4:31

APR. 12

REFLECTION. Often we are not sure how we should share our values with others. We feel bad when we timidly stand by when we see people making bad or self-destructive choices.

The Spirit gives us the wisdom and strength to say what is right, even if that means we will have to pay a price for doing it.

PRAYER. *May I be courageous, O Holy Spirit, in sharing the insights of my faith with others.*

HE one who sows in his flesh will reap a harvest of corruption, but the one who sows in the Spirit will reap from the Spirit . . . eternal life. —Gal 6:8

APR. 13

REFLECTION. One of the constant themes running through Sacred Scripture is that one must choose between two paths. One leads to life and the other leads to death.

Here, St. Paul speaks of that choice in terms of a choice between the flesh (what is worldly and materialistic) and the Spirit (what is spiritual and good).

PRAYER. *May I reject that which drags me down and embrace that which lifts me up to You, O Spirit of God.*

WHEN the Spirit from on high is poured down upon us, then the desert will become an orchard and the orchard a forest. —Isa 32:15

APR. 14

REFLECTION. When God created us, He intended for there to be an intimate bond between God and us, between ourselves and others, and between us and nature. Sin has damaged all of these bonds.

The Spirit's creative love heals those bonds. Even nature will flourish when we walk by the Spirit for we will be treating it with sacred respect.

PRAYER. *Spirit of Peace, bring healing to this fractured world.*

DO not cast me out from your presence, or take away from me your Holy Spirit. —Ps 51:13

APR. 15

REFLECTION. This psalm speaks of the fact that we are all sinners. We cannot hope to convert if the Lord does not give us the grace we need.

Here we beg God not to punish us by departing from our lives, for if He did, our lives (whether spiritual or physical) would be over.

PRAYER. *May I always be one with You, Lord, and may I always sense that You are near.*

HE Spirit helps us in our weakness. For we do not know how to pray as we should . . . —Rom 8:26a

APR. 16

REFLECTION. Many of us have experienced a period of time when it seemed as if our prayers had become mechanical. We didn't feel any consolation. We wondered if we were doing something wrong.

Sometimes God allows us to feel these things so that when we pray, we might pray for the right reason (to give of ourselves and not just to feel consolation from above).

PRAYER. *Lord, teach me to pray.*

N wisdom one finds a *subtle* spirit, one that is agile, clear, unstained and certain. —Wis 7:22

APR. 17

REFLECTION. The ways of the Spirit are not always obvious. The Spirit often speaks through the events of everyday life or the comments of people around us or even through a quiet voice in our hearts.

There are times that the Spirit is like a hurricane, other times that the Spirit is a gentle, quiet breeze.

PRAYER. *Spirit of God, open my eyes to Your wonders and my ears to Your mysteries.*

HOEVER has ears should listen to what the Spirit says . . . To anyone who is victorious, I will give the right to eat from the tree of life . . .

—Rev 2:7

APR. 18

REFLECTION. When we sinned, we deprived ourselves of the life that God intended us to have. Symbolically speaking, we were cast out of the Garden of Eden in which the tree of life was found.

If we die with Christ, we will inherit everlasting life—we will regain access to that tree. No fear of death, sin, illness or loneliness will ever have power over us again.

PRAYER. *Fill me with Your life, O life-giving Spirit of God.*

SPIRIT of *knowledge* and of fear of the Lord, and he shall delight in the fear of the Lord. —Isa 11:2-3

APR. 19

REFLECTION. Even if we were to study the wonders of the world until the day we died, we would never know them all. The Spirit reveals those things to us that help us grow in a spirit of awe and wonder.

We generally think that the Spirit reveals heavenly things, but through the Spirit we also come to understand the mysteries of this created world.

PRAYER. *May I know all that I can, and be humble enough to admit what I don't know.*

TO one, is given through the Spirit the utterance of wisdom; and to another, the utterance of knowledge . . .

—1 Cor 12:8

APR. 20

REFLECTION. Each of us is given the gifts of the Spirit (charisms) as we need them. We are supposed to use those gifts for our own growth but especially for the needs of the community.

But none of us has all the gifts, which is why we need to reach out to others in the community who have the gifts that we do not.

PRAYER. *May I use my gifts well, Spirit of God, and may I respect the gifts of others.*

SIGNS and wonders are known to wisdom as well as the plans of times and ages.

—Wis 8:8

APR. 21

REFLECTION. When one is given the Spirit of wisdom, one is able to perceive God's fingerprints upon the wonders of the world. One is able to see the pattern God has established in history (world history, faith history, and even our own personal history).

This should leave us with a sense of comfort, for it means that life is not chaotic. God has a plan.

PRAYER. *Let me discern Your plan, O Spirit, so that I may cooperate with it fully.*

OR the one whom God has sent speaks the words of God, for God gives Him the Spirit without measure. —Jn 3:34

APR. 22

REFLECTION. Jesus was the One Whom God sent, and Jesus proclaimed the Good News both in word and deed. He was extravagant in sharing His love, even to the point of being willing to die on the Cross.

Do I ration my availability when others need help?

PRAYER. *Give me a profound generosity of heart, O Spirit of God, so that I too might give of myself without measure.*

HEN Samson reaches Lehi, the Spirit of the Lord rushed upon him. The ropes around his arms became like flax consumed by the fire. —Jdg 15:14

APR. 23

REFLECTION. In the Old Testament, possession of the Spirit was associated with great strength and miraculous deeds.

Even today, we find a truth in this, for if we allow the Spirit to dwell in our hearts, then we will find peace and probably be better off physically because we will not be filled with anxiety and fear.

PRAYER. *Take possession of my heart, O Spirit of God, and fill me with Your peace.*

ET you hearts on the greater gifts. Now I will show you a more excellent way.
—1 Cor 12:31

APR. 24

REFLECTION. The Spirit of God showers many different charisms (gifts) upon us. Which are the most important gifts? We may think that it would be the gifts that are the most spectacular (e.g. healing, foretelling the future).

But the most important gifts are those which we can use to serve others. Love is the true measure of all things.

PRAYER. *Spirit of God, shower Your gifts upon me in abundance.*

HE Spirit of the Lord has spoken through me for His word was on my tongue.
—2 Sam 23:2

APR. 25

REFLECTION. What King David said about himself was also true for the evangelist St. Mark, and it should likewise be true for us today.

While we are not writing psalms or a Gospel, we do become living forms of God's Word when we allow the Spirit to speak through our lives (and we might be the only Gospel that many people ever read).

PRAYER. *May my life be a Gospel written to proclaim Your Good News to the world.*

HAT is too sublime for you, you should not seek, nor should you search after things beyond your strength. —Sir 3:20

APR. 26

REFLECTION. It is not a bad thing to know our limitations. Many, many things would be good, but we do not have the time or energy to do them all. Furthermore, some of our unrealistic expectations only lead us to frustration and resentment.

We can aim high in our lives, as long as we do it with a spirit of humility.

PRAYER. *Lord, guide me so that I know what can and should be done, and what should be left to another to do.*

WILL pour out upon the house of David and those who live in Jerusalem a spirit of grace and petition. —Zec 12:10

APR. 27

REFLECTION. When the Prophet speaks of the "house of David," he is speaking about the royal family.

By referring to them, the Prophet is saying that the Spirit will come upon everyone in Jerusalem, from the most powerful to the least significant. They will all recognize how much they need the grace of the Lord.

PRAYER. *May we all recognize our need for You, O Spirit of God, and reach out to You without reserve.*

HEN he [Barnabas] arrived and perceived the grace of God, he rejoiced . . . for he was a good man, filled with the Holy Spirit and faith.

—Acts 11:23-24

APR. 28

REFLECTION. Barnabas, being a good and faith-filled man, was able to recognize how God was working through the Christians in Antioch.

They were doing things in a new way, but rather than reject what was new and unfamiliar, Barnabas discerned that this was the work of the Spirit and he rejoiced.

PRAYER. *Holy Spirit, teach me to be open to the ways You renew the world and the Church in every age.*

HIS is how you can recognize the Spirit of God: every spirit that acknowledges that Jesus Christ came in the flesh is from God. **—1 Jn 4:2**

APR. 29

REFLECTION. Some people in John's community had denied that Jesus could be God because they thought that what was spiritual was good and what was material was bad.

Yet, when God created this world He pronounced it to be good, and Jesus Himself was born in the flesh.

PRAYER. *May I encounter You in spiritual revelations, God, but may I also recognize Your presence in the world around me.*

OU will receive power when the Holy Spirit comes upon you, and then you will be my witnesses . . . —Acts 1:8

APR. 30

REFLECTION. The Spirit calls us to share our faith with those who are near and far.

It could be as simple as giving witness in our everyday lives. Or it might involve a vocation to go to a foreign land or at least to support missionaries who do that in Christ's name.

PRAYER. *Come, O Holy Spirit, and commission me to proclaim the Word of God.*

OU are to trust in the Lord with all your heart and not rely upon your own intelligence. —Prov 3:5

MAY 1

REFLECTION. There are limits to how much we can know, and it is good to recognize this.

When we rely too much upon our own efforts, we can fool ourselves. We can mistake selfish preferences for moral choices, intellectual speculation for the truth. When we allow God to guide us, we live in the truth.

PRAYER. *Let my heart be humble, O Lord, and my spirit be meek.*

BELOVED, do not trust every spirit, but test the spirits to see whether they are from God. —1 Jn 4:1

MAY 2

REFLECTION. Many people claim that they have a message from God to share with us. Some of them are authentic, while others are only proclaiming their own pet ideas.

We should ask whether their ideas coincide with what the Church has believed from the beginning.

PRAYER. *Give me insight, Spirit of Wisdom, so that I may be able to discern that which is from You and that which is not.*

THEN the Spirit said to Philip, "Go up and join that chariot" [the chariot of the Ethiopian eunuch]. —Acts 8:29

MAY 3

REFLECTION. In the Old Testament, eunuchs were excluded from the people of Israel because of their lack of physical integrity.

The Holy Spirit, by sending Philip to this Ethiopian eunuch, is proclaiming that all are invited to belong to the people of God.

PRAYER. *Send me, Spirit of God, to reach out to those who have so often been rejected and unloved.*

EFLECT on the precepts of the Lord . . . then He will enlighten your mind and grant you the wisdom you desire.

—Sir 6:37

MAY 4

REFLECTION. God's law is not just a set of laws imposed on us from above. It is a gift from God to guide us in the right path.

Do I examine my conscience every day to make God's law my own?

PRAYER. *Speak to my heart, O Spirit of God, and guide me in Your ways.*

N wisdom there is a *firm* spirit, one that is secure and tranquil.

—Wis 7:23

MAY 5

REFLECTION. Everything seems to be changing today. Even morality seems to be flexible and relative.

It is the Spirit Who reminds us that God's ways and God's will are not negotiable. God is the same yesterday, today, and tomorrow.

PRAYER. *Be a firm anchor in my life, O Comforter, a tranquil harbor in which I find refuge.*

CONFESS your sins to one another and pray for one another, so that you may be healed. —Jas 5:16

MAY 6

REFLECTION. The Holy Spirit is the instrument of God's love and healing. God's love brings us forgiveness of our sins. That same Spirit can also bring us healing from our brokenness (those things which make it easier for us to fall into sin).

Only love can heal us, and the Spirit bestows that healing on us in abundance.

PRAYER. *Forgive my sins, O Lord, and heal my brokenness.*

THE Spirit himself bears witness with our Spirit that we are children of God. —Rom 8:16

MAY 7

REFLECTION. The Spirit of God speaks within the depths of our being to our own spirit to reveal to us what God thinks of us. God considers us to be His beloved children.

When we pray to the Father and desire to experience a good, loving, compassionate parent, we are already hearing Who God is for the Spirit is telling us to hope for this very thing.

PRAYER. *Abba! Father! Guide me and comfort me.*

OD is Spirit, and those who worship Him must worship in Spirit and truth.

—Jn 4:24

MAY 8

REFLECTION. We worship God the Father in Spirit and in Truth. For Christians, the Spirit is the Holy Spirit. For us, the Truth is Jesus. Thus, we pray to God the Father in and through the Holy Spirit and Jesus.

We even hear this in the closing doxology of the Eucharistic Prayer.

PRAYER. *Through him, and with him, and in him, O God, almighty Father, in the unity of the Holy Spirit, all glory and honor is yours, for ever and ever.*

HEN the Spirit of the Lord left Saul, he began to be tormented by an evil spirit sent by the Lord.

—1 Sam 16:14

MAY 9

REFLECTION. When King Saul sinned, he was rejecting the Spirit of Truth in his heart. He opened himself to the action of spirits that were opposed to God's goodness, e.g. the spirit of jealousy and rage.

Sin suffocates the breath of the Spirit in our lives; conversion renews that life and love in our hearts.

PRAYER. *Holy Spirit, help me to reject whatever is evil and choose only what is good.*

THE Lord has anointed me; He has commissioned me to bring glad tidings to the lonely and to heal the brokenhearted.
—Isa 61:1a

MAY 10

REFLECTION. The Holy Spirit anointed St. Damien to be a missionary to the lepers.

Damien brought them the Word of God which he preached with word and with his life. When he contracted leprosy, he became one with them, thus destroying the isolation they had experienced because of their illness.

PRAYER. *Lord, may I reach out to the lepers of my age.*

WHEN you take away their breath, they die and return to the dust.
—Ps 104:29

MAY 11

REFLECTION. God breathed into Adam and made him into a living being. If God takes back that breath, he (we) will return to the dust from which we were created.

When we sin, we deny that Spirit's presence within us. We reject our God-given destiny and act as if we were still nothing more than dirt.

PRAYER. *Breathe Your Spirit back into my heart, O God, through Your sacraments and Your other signs of love.*

SHALL acknowledge his name in the presence of my Father and his Angels. Whoever has ears should listen to what the Spirit says.
—Rev 3:5-6

MAY 12

REFLECTION. Some people are afraid that when they die, God may hold some sin against them that they forgot to confess or had not even known was a sin. Yet, Jesus promises us that if we hold on to Him and give witness to His truth, He will stand as a witness on our behalf.

The Holy Spirit reminds us that God does not expect perfection, only fidelity.

PRAYER. *I believe in You, Lord, and I love You.*

LL the ways of a person might be pure in that person's eyes, but it is the Lord Who can discern the tenor of one's spirit. **—Prov 16:2**

MAY 13

REFLECTION. There are times that we don't even realize our hidden motivations. We rationalize, we become defensive, we deny, and yet those motivations sooner or later catch up with us.

The Spirit helps us sort through the fog of our minds and hearts so that we might live in the truth.

PRAYER. *May the only estimation that I am concerned with be Yours, O Lord.*

THEN they cast lots for them, and the lot fell to Matthias, who was then added to the eleven Apostles. —Acts 1:26

MAY 14

REFLECTION. It was important to the Apostles that they allow themselves to be guided by the Holy Spirit. When it was time to replace Judas Iscariot, they chose two appropriate candidates and allowed the Holy Spirit to make the final choice.

How does the Holy Spirit work in the decisions of who will guide our Church, e.g. Pope, bishops, etc.?

PRAYER. *Loving Spirit of God, always give us the leaders we need in our Church and our world.*

AMONG wisdom's treasures is the example of prudence, but fear of the Lord is considered to be an abomination to the sinner. —Sir 1:22

MAY 15

REFLECTION. We usually associate the action of the Spirit with power and exuberance, not with prudence. Yet, the Spirit teaches us how to be prudent and loving when we use our spiritual gifts.

In the Spirit, we become vessels of God's grace without appropriating the honor and glory to ourselves.

PRAYER. *Gentle Spirit, may I always be prudent in what I say and do.*

AIT quietly for the Lord, be patient until He comes.

—Ps 37:7

MAY 16

REFLECTION. In our fast-paced world, we want instant answers and complete solutions to our problems. But often, especially when we are discerning what the Spirit wants of us, we must wait and listen attentively.

Silence is sometimes already an answer: telling us to be quiet and wait in patience.

PRAYER. *Spirit of God, teach me to patiently wait for Your time.*

N wisdom there is a *manifold* spirit that is subtle, agile and clear . . .

—Wis 7:22

MAY 17

REFLECTION. We speak of the seven gifts of the Holy Spirit. Seven is the perfect number in the Bible. By speaking of seven gifts, we are really saying that the Spirit is manifested in many, many different ways.

What are some of the gifts of the Spirit that I already have and what are some that I desire?

PRAYER. *Gracious Holy Spirit, grant me an abundant share in Your many gifts.*

THE heavens were made by the word of the Lord, and all their host by the breath of His mouth. —Ps 33:6

MAY 18

REFLECTION. The ancients understood that words are powerful. They can heal hearts or break spirits. God's word and life-giving Spirit created the universe and hold them in being.

By listening to God's word and by opening our hearts to His Spirit, we are recreated in His love.

PRAYER. *Speak Your word into my heart, O Spirit of God.*

IN wisdom there is an *unhampered spirit* that is beneficent and kindly . . . —Wis 7:22-23

MAY 19

REFLECTION. The Holy Spirit can transform any situation into an opportunity for grace. Even the tragedy of sin is an opportunity for the Spirit to respond with pardon and mercy.

The Spirit invites us to look at what happens in our lives in a similar manner—to see everything as an opportunity for love and patience and healing and compassion.

PRAYER. *Holy Spirit, may I see everything that happens in my life as an opportunity for grace.*

HEN the Spirit of the Lord possessed Samson, he went down to Ashkelon and killed thirty of the enemy . . . **—Jdg 14:19**

MAY 20

REFLECTION. Was the Holy Spirit really the one who impelled Samson to kill the Philistines? Or was the Spirit simply commanding Samson to protect his people, and Samson, living in dangerous times, interpreted this message as one of violence.

None of these questions can find an answer except in the life and teachings of Jesus.

PRAYER. *Spirit of peace and love, teach me Your ways.*

N contrast, the fruit of the Spirit is . . . *faithfulness*, gentleness, and self-control. **—Gal 5:22-23**

MAY 21

REFLECTION. One of the attributes most frequently posited for Yahweh in the Old Testament is faithfulness or fidelity. God never turns His back on His promises.

The Spirit helps us to be faithful as well, people of integrity who embrace their commitments without reservation or compromise.

PRAYER. *Make me a person of my word, O God, as faithful to my commitments as You are to Yours.*

OD created humans in His image, in His divine image He created them, male and female He created them.

—Gen 1:27

MAY 22

REFLECTION. We are created in God's image and likeness. We carry the breath of the Holy Spirit in our hearts and souls. God has given us an incredible dignity.

We must live in that dignity, not settling for anything that would make us less than what God intended us to be.

PRAYER. *May I never do anything that negates the dignity with which You created me.*

HE law of the spirit of life in Christ Jesus has set you free from the law of sin and death. **—Rom 8:2**

MAY 23

REFLECTION. When Christ is the center of our lives, we are fully alive. When He is not, we easily slip into bad choices that lead to sin and selfishness and spiritual death. That is not true freedom; it is a form of slavery to our passions.

True freedom is found in choosing to live and love in Christ.

PRAYER. *Free me, Holy Spirit, from my enslavement to my passions.*

EHOLD, I am making my words a fire in your mouth. And this people is the wood that it will devour. —Jer 5:14

MAY 24

REFLECTION. While many of the Prophets preached consolation to the people of Israel, Jeremiah preached judgment and destruction. Things had gotten so bad that God needed to bring His people to their senses with a violent intervention.

Jeremiah did this because he truly loved them and could not stand by while they destroyed themselves spiritually.

PRAYER. *Spirit of God, console me with Your love and challenge me with Your truth.*

F one yearns for abundant learning, wisdom knows the things of old and infers those that are yet to come. —Wis 8:8a

MAY 25

REFLECTION. In the Old Testament, it was believed that it was Wisdom that helped us make sense of things. In the light of the New Testament, we realize that it is the Holy Spirit.

St. Bede wrote about Christian history to show how the Holy Spirit guided the Church in the past, present, and even into the future.

PRAYER. *Eternal, unchanging God, help us to see Your presence in the events of our time.*

HE Holy Spirit also testifies to us about this. For He first says, "This is the covenant that I will make with them. . . ." —Heb 10:15-16

MAY 26

REFLECTION. St. Philip Neri preached on the love and compassion of the Lord. He invited many people to renew their commitment to their faith through a more profound celebration of the Sacraments of Reconciliation and the Eucharist.

Do I renew my covenant with God periodically? Every day?

PRAYER. *Make my faith ever new, O Spirit of Faithfulness, and may it constantly grow through my participation in the sacraments.*

WILL put My Spirit within you and make you live by My statutes, careful to observe My decrees. —Ezek 36:27

MAY 27

REFLECTION. Ezekiel the Prophet was very discouraged by the fact that his people had been so unfaithful to the Lord. He spoke of a time when God would establish a new covenant with them that would be internalized, written not on stone but on their hearts.

The Spirit of God would revitalize their commitment to be the people of the Lord.

PRAYER. *Holy Spirit, renew Your covenant in my heart.*

HE showers down knowledge and full understanding; she heightens the glory of those who possess her. —Sir 1:17

MAY 28

REFLECTION. Glory is usually a word associated with God, but when the Spirit of God fills our hearts with knowledge and understanding, we recognize that we share in God's glory.

Furthermore, we express that glory by living a virtue-filled life.

PRAYER. *Spirit of Holiness, sanctify me in Your virtue.*

OHN baptized with water, but within a few days you will be baptized with the Holy Spirit. —Acts 1:5

MAY 29

REFLECTION. The baptism of John the Baptist was a baptism of repentance.

Christian baptism brings us forgiveness of our sins, but it also brings us an adoption as children of God. The Spirit invites us into the life of the Trinity.

PRAYER. *Every time I bless myself with holy water may I recommit myself to my baptismal promises.*

EAR the prayers of Your servants, for You are always gracious to Your people. —Sir 36:15

MAY 30

REFLECTION. All throughout the Old Testament, the Prophets and sages celebrated the generosity of God to His people. We often count the cost of our commitments. God does not hold back.

Is this the way we should act when we are asked to help others? When are we called to be prudent and careful, and when are we called to be outrageously generous?

PRAYER. *Holy Spirit, guide me to treat others as You wish them to be treated.*

HEN Elizabeth heard Mary's greeting, the baby leaped in her womb. Then Elizabeth was filled with the Holy Spirit . . . —Lk 1:41-42

MAY 31

REFLECTION. It is the Spirit Who gives us the ability to know the truth about others.

When we look at them from a human point of view, we will tend to concentrate on their flaws and shortcomings. When we view them in a spiritual way, we will see what truly lies in their hearts.

PRAYER. *Spirit of God, may I always see people as You see them.*

IT was revealed to them that they were serving not themselves but you when they spoke of the things . . . —1 Pet 1:12

JUNE 1

REFLECTION. The Prophets often thought that they were only speaking about things that were occurring in their own days, but the Holy Spirit had a second level of meaning in mind. That level pointed to Jesus and His ministry.

Likewise, the Holy Spirit gives a second level of meaning to what happens to us as well, a level that is based upon our faith.

PRAYER. *May I always remember, O Lord, that Your Spirit is working below the surface of what is happening in my life.*

SO they [Paul and Barnabas] shook the dust from their feet in protest against them . . . And the disciples were filled with joy and with the Holy Spirit. —Acts 13:51-52

JUNE 2

REFLECTION. Rejection and joy are usually not associated with each other, but Paul and Barnabas had been given the responsibility of preaching the Good News. They rejoiced that they were found worthy to suffer for that Word.

Their suffering was not a defeat, it was a privilege.

PRAYER. *When I suffer, O Spirit of God, may I be filled with Your peace and joy.*

F you are reviled for the name of Christ, consider yourself blessed, for upon you rests the Spirit of glory and of God.

—1 Pet 4:14

JUNE 3

REFLECTION. Charles Lwanga and his companions were so Spirit-filled that they refused to renounce their faith in order to save their lives. They were virtuous men.

Rather than being defeated by their martyrdom, they conquered the powers of evil by living in faith, hope and charity.

PRAYER. *Teach me Your virtue, Spirit of God, and give me the courage to live in it.*

E, ourselves, who have the first-fruits of the Spirit, groan inwardly as we wait for our adoption as children, the redemption of our bodies.

—Rom 8:23

JUNE 4

REFLECTION. When Jesus died on the Cross and rose from the dead, He freed us from our slavery to sin.

Yet, His promise that we can live in God's love is not yet fully actualized, for we are still living upon this earth and we still sin. Therefore, we groan, longing for that day when we shall be one with God.

PRAYER. *Fill me with the gift of Your Spirit, Lord, and increase my desire to be one with You.*

ISDOM is a kindly spirit, yet she does not acquit a blasphemer who has guilty lips.

—Wis 1:6

JUNE 5

REFLECTION. Being kind and merciful does not mean that we should overlook the sins of others. True mercy is first of all honest for that which is not acknowledged cannot be healed. The Spirit allows us to be brutally honest with ourselves and compassionately honest with others so that we can turn back to the Lord.

Do I run away from confrontation (with myself and others) to preserve the illusion of peace?

PRAYER. *Holy Spirit, help me to reject whatever is evil and choose only what is good.*

HE Lord God does not do anything without first revealing His plans to the prophets, His servants. —Am 3:7

JUNE 6

REFLECTION. God has called us to be His friends and His co-workers in the plan of salvation.

Although He is God and we are only creatures, Jesus tells us that we are not slaves. We are His friends, for He reveals to us Who He is and what He wants from us.

PRAYER. *May my every word and action cooperate with Your plan, O God, to build up the kingdom.*

F I pray in a tongue, my spirit is at prayer but my mind derives no benefit.

—1 Cor 14:14

JUNE 7

REFLECTION. When Paul speaks of praying in tongues, he is speaking about unintelligible utterances. The person is so Spirit-filled that regular words no longer suffice.

As good as this gift is, it is not enough for one is not helping the Church when no one understands what the person is saying.

PRAYER. *Give me the right words, O Gracious Spirit, to proclaim Your truth to the world.*

HE fruit of the Spirit is found in love, joy, peace, patience, kindness, generosity, faithfulness, gentleness and self-control. **—Gal 5:22-23**

JUNE 8

REFLECTION. St. Paul wanted to distinguish between the disorder that comes into our lives when we live by our passions and the ordered, disciplined lives we find when we live in the Spirit. This is why his list of passions is confused and disordered while this list of virtues is ordered in three sets of three.

Is my life-style well ordered or chaotic?

PRAYER. *Spirit of God, fill my life with a sense of Your guidance, with an abundance of Your gifts.*

ISDOM can understand the turn of a phrase and can solve riddles.
—Wis 8:8b

JUNE 9

REFLECTION. In the Old Testament, the Spirit of wisdom does not only refer to spiritual realities. It also refers to a cleverness in which one knows the turn of a phrase or the solution to riddles.

Cleverness was considered to be a highly esteemed virtue in the ancient Middle East, which is why Jesus counseled His followers to be clever in both worldly and spiritual things.

PRAYER. *Spirit of God, teach me to be clever as a serpent but innocent as a dove.*

SPIRIT of *wisdom and understanding* as well as a spirit of counsel and strength . . .
—Isa 11:2

JUNE 10

REFLECTION. According to Isaiah, the coming Messiah would be endowed with the spirit of wisdom and understanding. Those whom God has placed in positions of authority need these gifts if they are to govern well.

We are called to pray for those who lead our Church and our country.

PRAYER. *O Holy Spirit, grant Your wisdom and understanding to our leaders.*

BUT there is a spirit in humans, the breath of the Almighty that gives people understanding.
—Job 32:8

JUNE 11

REFLECTION. When God breathed His Spirit into Adam, it was not only to make him a living creature. That same Holy Spirit also gave him insight into the things of God.

We, as creatures, cannot hope to understand the mysteries of our faith on our own, but with the gift of the Spirit we have an insight into those mysteries from within our own hearts.

PRAYER. *Speak to my heart, O Spirit of God, and instruct me in mysteries of our faith.*

IN wisdom one finds a spirit that pervades all other spirits.
—Wis 7:23

JUNE 12

REFLECTION. The Bible speaks of many spirits, some of which are holy and others evil. Wisdom helps us discern what truly comes from God and what is the product of other spirits: pride, jealousy, arrogance, self-righteousness, bitterness, etc.

Wisdom makes transparent the hidden motives of our hearts.

PRAYER. *Pour out Your Spirit of Holiness upon me, O Lord, so that my motives might be pure.*

HE Spirit of the Lord God has come upon me for the Lord has anointed me . . . to announce good news to the oppressed. —Isa 61:1

JUNE 13

REFLECTION. St. Anthony of Padua's spirit-filled preaching brought great consolation to those who heard him. It challenged them to conversion and offered them love and healing.

We cannot experience true consolation until we change our ways so that we might be receptive to God's message to us.

PRAYER. *Anoint me, Lord, as You anointed St. Anthony with the Spirit of Wisdom.*

OR as it is written, "Eye has not seen, ear has not heard" . . . yet, God has revealed these things to us through the Spirit. —1 Cor 2:9-10

JUNE 14

REFLECTION. When we look at the wonders of nature, we can learn something about the God Who created these things. When we consider the movements of history, we can discern what God has in mind for us.

Yet, there are many mysteries about God that we could never figure out on our own. It is only through the Spirit that we can enter into those mysteries.

PRAYER. *Reveal Your mysteries to me, Spirit of Wisdom, so that I may live in Your love.*

AS the four horses patrolled out upon the earth, He called out to me and said, "Behold, they go forth . . . to make My Spirit dwell in the land of the north."

—Zec 6:7-8

JUNE 15

REFLECTION. The four horses are types of envoys who search the earth to report to God what is happening on it. No place is hidden from God's eyes or can escape His plan.

God still keeps a watch over us for He cares for us and does not want to lose any of us.

PRAYER. *Keep guard over my thoughts, Holy Spirit, and watch over my every word and action.*

HE makes the past and the future known and reveals the deepest secrets. He lacks no understanding, nothing escapes Him. —Sir 42:19-20

JUNE 16

REFLECTION. The Holy Spirit helps us to understand the meaning of history, whether it be salvation history or our own personal history.

Although God exists in eternity, He controls the events of time to conform to His plan which leads to the salvation of those whom He loves.

PRAYER. *May I use every minute of my time as a precious gift from You, O Lord, and never miss an opportunity to do good in Your name.*

N all of your prayers and entreaties, pray always in the Holy Spirit.

—Eph 6:18

JUNE 17

REFLECTION. There are many opportunities throughout the day to turn to prayer. Even moments of temptation (e.g. to anger, to jealousy, to judgmentalism, etc.) can be opportunities to pray for those whom we would be ready to reject.

Everything and every moment is an opportunity to open our hearts to the Spirit of prayer.

PRAYER. *May I pray always and everywhere, never ceasing to praise and to thank You, to ask for Your pardon and to seek Your assistance.*

HE hand of the Lord was upon me, and I was led out in the Spirit of the Lord. He guided me to the center of a plain that was filled with bones. —Ezek 37:1

JUNE 18

REFLECTION. When the Spirit led the Prophet Ezekiel out into a bone-filled field (which was probably a type of cemetery), it helped him see a great truth of our faith.

Ezekiel came to understand that God would raise us up from the dead on the Last Day.

PRAYER. *Raise us up, O Lord, into the glory of Your kingdom.*

HOEVER has ears should listen to what the Spirit says . . . To anyone who is victorious, I will give some of the hidden manna. —Rev 2:17a

JUNE 19

REFLECTION. In the Old Testament, manna was the food that God gave to the Israelites in the desert. Some of the manna was stored in the Ark of the Covenant that Jews believed would reappear on the Day of the Lord.

For Christians, the hidden manna is the fact that the Eucharist is the Body and Blood of Jesus. On the Day of the Lord, we will see Jesus face to face.

PRAYER. *Feed me with Your manna, Lord. Nourish the deepest hunger of my heart.*

HOSE who fear You will rejoice when they see me because I place my hope in Your word. —Ps 119:74

JUNE 20

REFLECTION. A Spirit-filled person will always be joyful when that person sees another living in God's ways. It will be seen as a sign of the dawning of the Kingdom of God.

Our job as Christians is not only to reject what is evil, but also to celebrate the triumph of good in ourselves and others.

PRAYER. *Fill my heart with optimism, Holy Spirit, so that I can see how Your goodness is already triumphing in the world.*

MAY wisdom visit me and guide me, so that I might know what You desire. —Wis 9:10b

JUNE 21

REFLECTION. This is a form of the prayer that King Solomon raised up to the Lord. He realized that no matter how much goodwill he had, he could not reign successfully on his own.

He needed the gift of wisdom from the Holy Spirit in order to govern God's people with justice and compassion.

PRAYER. *May Your wisdom visit me as well, O Spirit of God, and guide me in all my ways.*

AS long as I have life and the breath of God in my nostrils, my lips will not utter falsehoods nor my tongue deceit. —Job 27:3-4

JUNE 22

REFLECTION. The Spirit is a Spirit of truth. We cannot afford to tell half truths or "little white lies," let alone larger, more serious lies.

The goal is to be so transparent that if people could read the secret thoughts of our hearts, we would not be embarrassed by what they might see.

PRAYER. *May my every thought and my every word be righteous and loving.*

HE grass will wither and the flowers wilt whenever the breath of the Lord blows upon them. —Isa 40:7

JUNE 23

REFLECTION. Normally, the breath of God's Spirit brings life. But in the hot desert, wind blows over the plants of the field and causes them to wither.

If we cooperate with God's grace, we grow in holiness. If we fight against the inspiration of the Spirit, then God's life within us withers away and dies.

PRAYER. *Let Your breath upon me, O Holy Spirit, bring healing and life.*

E will be filled with the Holy Spirit, and he will bring back many of the people of Israel to the Lord their God. —Lk 1:15-16

JUNE 24

REFLECTION. John the Baptist preached repentance so that his listeners might be ready to embrace the Messiah.

The Holy Spirit invites each of us to examine the choices we make in our lives so that we, like the people of Israel, may be willing to turn from our bad habits and selfish ways and embrace God's ways.

PRAYER. *Lead me back to You, O Spirit of God, for You are my refuge and strength.*

SPIRIT of knowledge and of the *fear of the Lord*, and his delight shall be the fear of the Lord.

—Isa 11:2-3

JUNE 25

REFLECTION. Fear of the Lord does not mean to be afraid of God. St. John tells us that where there is love, there is no fear.

Rather, fear of the Lord is to stand in awe and wonder before the greatness of the Lord. It is to recognize that God is the creator and we are the creatures. Fear of the Lord should lead us to praise and worship.

PRAYER. *May You be praised and glorified, Lord, in all Your grandeur.*

ISDOM hastens to make herself known to those who desire her.

—Wis 6:12

JUNE 26

REFLECTION. God's wisdom and the other gifts of the Spirit are not inaccessible to us. God is so generous that He pours those gifts upon anyone who seeks them.

It is not that we can force God's hand, but we can prepare ourselves to embrace the bounty of the Lord.

PRAYER. *Prepare my heart, O Generous Spirit of God, for the outpouring of Your gifts.*

N wisdom there is a *certain* Spirit that is not baneful and loves the good . . .

—Wis 7:22

JUNE 27

REFLECTION. "To be or not to be?" These words from Hamlet have given the nickname of "Hamlet" to someone who can't make up his mind. A Hamlet is afraid of committing, of taking a risk.

The Spirit takes an outrageous risk on each one of us by loving us beyond measure. That same Spirit invites us to take the risk of living lives of pure love.

PRAYER. *Let me take the ultimate risk on Your love, O Holy Spirit, in the certainty that You will be faithful to Your promise.*

OWEVER, it is God Who enables both us and you to stand firm in Christ.

—2 Cor 1:21

JUNE 28

REFLECTION. How do we know that God loves us? How do we know if we're doing the right thing? It is the Holy Spirit Who gives us that assurance.

We no longer feel tossed around by every new idea or fear. We know to the deepest core of our being that all is well.

PRAYER. *Spirit of God, let me feel Your presence and know Your consolation each day of my life.*

HESE are the two olive trees and the two lampstands that stand in the presence of the Lord . . . —Rev 11:4

JUNE 29

REFLECTION. There are two witnesses in this text (for two are needed to give witness). They are lampstands (which are symbols for the Church).

They burn oil, a symbol of the power of the Holy Spirit. These witnesses are so filled with the Spirit that they are also olive trees; they will never run out of this gift.

PRAYER. *Shower Your gift of the Spirit down upon Your Church, O Lord, so that we might be as courageous in giving witness as were Saints Peter and Paul.*

E must always give thanks to God for you . . . because God chose you from the beginning to be saved through sanctification by the Spirit . . . —2 Thes 2:13

JUNE 30

REFLECTION. The early Christian martyrs could only have had the courage to die for the faith if they were filled with the assurance and courage of the Holy Spirit. Otherwise, they would have judged their deaths to be a defeat.

In the Spirit, they came to realize that the blood of the martyrs is the seed of the Church.

PRAYER. *May I live a life of witness to my faith, even if that means I must pay a price.*

THE Advocate, the Holy Spirit whom the Father will send in My name, will teach you everything and remind you of all that I have said to you. —Jn 14:26

JULY 1

REFLECTION. The mysteries of God are far beyond our understanding.

Yet, the Holy Spirit both reveals what we could never have known on our own and helps us to understand what we have already heard but have not yet comprehended.

PRAYER. *Revealing Spirit of God, teach me Your truths so that I might understand Your wonders.*

AS for you, the anointing you received from Him remains in you, and therefore you do not need anyone to teach you. —1 Jn 2:27a

JULY 2

REFLECTION. When we are open to the action of the Holy Spirit, we learn the truth about God in our hearts. That is why things simply make sense to us when we hear or read them.

Yet, that gift in our hearts always has to be balanced with the voice of the Spirit speaking through the Magisterium.

PRAYER. *Speak to my heart, O Holy Spirit, and speak to me through those You have chosen to guide Your Church.*

N wisdom there is a *secure* spirit that is tranquil, all-powerful and all-seeing . . .
—Wis 7:23

JULY 3

REFLECTION. In a world in which everything seems to be changeable and in which we are not always sure of what is right, the Spirit is a stable and sure foundation for our beliefs.

When we have doubts like St. Thomas the Apostle had, the Spirit encourages us and strengthens us so that we may believe.

PRAYER. *When I have doubts, O Holy Spirit, fill my heart with Your certainty.*

Y his powerful spirit Isaiah examined the future and consoled the mourners of Zion.
—Sir 48:24

JULY 4

REFLECTION. There are times that we need to know that our present difficulties will not last forever. We need to remember that with God anything is possible.

The Spirit gives us this perspective for the Spirit fills us with hope (which does not mean that everything will work out, but rather that God will never abandon us).

PRAYER. *Teach me to hope, Holy Spirit, even when hope does not seem to be possible.*

OD also testified to it by signs and wonders and various miracles, and by gifts of the Holy Spirit distributed according to His will. **—Heb 2:4**

JULY 5

REFLECTION. All throughout Jesus' ministry, He pointed to the Father as the giver of all good gifts. This includes the gifts of the Holy Spirit.

Jesus and the Holy Spirit are obedient to the will of the Father. Obedience is not subservience. It is fulfilling the will of Him Who wants what is best for us.

PRAYER. *Like Jesus and the Spirit, O Father, may I be obedient to Your will.*

IMPLORE you by the mercies of God to offer your bodies as a living sacrifice that is holy and acceptable to God—a spiritual act of worship. **—Rom 12:1**

JULY 6

REFLECTION. Our bodies are the temples of the Holy Spirit. We are to treat them with dignity and respect. St. Maria Goretti serves as an example of this for she preferred to die rather than to allow her body to be defiled.

Do I treat my body with respect with what I eat, how I exercise and recreate, etc.?

PRAYER. *May I offer up my body as a gift to You, God, one that is both precious and pure.*

IS head and His hair were white . . . and His eyes were like a burning flame. —Rev 1:14

JULY 7

REFLECTION. White hair may be a sign of age and wisdom. The Son of Man shares in the ancient wisdom of the Father.

Eyes in the Bible stand for the action of the Holy Spirit. The Son of Man's fiery eyes mean that He is Spirit-filled, able to see into our hearts and souls.

PRAYER. *See into my heart, O Spirit of God, and heal that which is not filled with Your love.*

O not quench the Spirit. Do not despise prophecies. —1 Thes 5:19-20

JULY 8

REFLECTION. The Spirit often speaks in ways we would not have expected and through people whom we would be tempted to distrust.

We cannot close our minds and hearts to the voice of the Spirit speaking through them lest we deprive ourselves of the Spirit's wisdom.

PRAYER. *May I be open to the ways that You speak in our times, O Spirit of God.*

OU, however, do not live according to the flesh but according to the Spirit, for the Spirit of God dwells in you.
—Rom 8:9

JULY 9

REFLECTION. St. Paul contrasts the flesh with the spirit. By "the flesh," he does not mean our material bodies and the world of creation. He means that part of us which can drag us down, our earthiness, or what St. Augustine called our concupiscence.

We have to reject those tendencies if we want to be open to the action of the Spirit.

PRAYER. *Purify my heart, O God, so that I may live by the Spirit and not by the flesh.*

N wisdom there is a *unique* spirit that is manifold, subtle and agile . . .
—Wis 7:22

JULY 10

REFLECTION. In Greek philosophy, things that were copies were not considered to be as good as things that were totally unique. The Holy Spirit is unlike any other spirit in goodness and holiness and generosity, etc.

We should not consult other spirits (e.g., through horoscopes or magic or psychics) for they are neither as powerful nor as good as the Spirit of God.

PRAYER. *May I choose You and only You, Spirit of God, to guide me in my ways.*

THE grace of our Lord Jesus Christ, the love of God and the fellowship of the Holy Spirit be with you all.

—2 Cor 13:13

JULY 11

REFLECTION. All three words: grace, love and fellowship, are basically the same thing. They represent the intimate relationship between the persons of the Trinity.

If we are one with God, we will also live in communion with those around us. Our relationships, in fact, should be based upon that of the persons of the Trinity.

PRAYER. *May my every relationship reflect the generosity of spirit exhibited by the persons of the Trinity.*

DO you suppose that it is without reason that Scripture says, "He yearns jealously for the Spirit that He sent to live in us?"

—Jas 4:5

JULY 12

REFLECTION. There are some people who believe that anything goes, that one idea is as good as the others. The Spirit reminds us that we cannot say "yes" to everything.

Sometimes we have to reject false ideas so that we might better live in the truth.

PRAYER. *Let me always say "yes" to You and "no" to that which leads me away from You.*

DID He not make them one flesh and spirit. You must then . . . not break faith with the wife of your youth.

—Mal 2:15

JULY 13

REFLECTION. God created Adam and Eve to be of mutual support to each other.

When people marry, they are uniting with each other body and soul and they are making a holy covenant with each other. The Prophet Malachi saw divorce as a physical and spiritual violation of this sacred commitment.

PRAYER. *Holy Spirit, please heal those marriages that are going through difficulties.*

THE fruit of the Spirit is . . . *generosity*, faithfulness, gentleness and self-control.

—Gal 5:22-23

JULY 14

REFLECTION. The Spirit, being the love between the Father and the Son, is pure generosity, pure giving of self to the other.

When we live in the Spirit, we only want to share the love with which God has loved us and share the material blessings we have received through the goodness of God.

PRAYER. *May I be generous in what I have and who I am, O gracious Gift of the Most High.*

I PRAYED, and prudence was given me. I begged, and the spirit of wisdom came upon me. —Wis 7:7

JULY 15

REFLECTION. Solomon prayed for prudence and wisdom so that he might govern God's people rightly. Because his request was unselfish, God granted what he sought.

When we pray, we should make sure that our desires are not motivated by selfishness. We should only want those gifts that help us most to serve others.

PRAYER. *Grant me, Holy Spirit, the gifts that will make me more generous and loving.*

SUDDENLY, there came from heaven a sound similar to that of a violent wind, and it filled the entire house . . . —Acts 2:2

JULY 16

REFLECTION. In the early chapters of Genesis, we hear that a strong wind/the Spirit of God hovered over the chaos. (Remember the Hebrew word for wind could also be translated as Spirit.)

Now, in the new creation of Pentecost, we hear about that mighty wind/Holy Spirit again. God is giving Mary and the Apostles a new, more profound life.

PRAYER. *Recreate my heart, O Promise of the Father, and renew the world in Your love.*

AKE love your aim, but strive earnestly after the spiritual gifts, especially for that of prophecy.

—1 Cor 14:1

JULY 17

REFLECTION. To prophesy means to see things from God's own point of view. This is an essential gift for the community for we need people who will give us this perspective.

And yet this gift and all other spiritual gifts are to be used with love.

PRAYER. *Revealing Spirit of God, guide us through the insights given to us through Your Prophets in our community.*

LL those who keep His commandments abide in Him, and He abides in them. —1 Jn 3:24

JULY 18

REFLECTION. There is an interior and an exterior dimension to our faith. The interior dimension is that we have the Spirit of God in our hearts, a Spirit Who teaches us Who God is and what God wants of us.

The exterior dimension is that we keep God's commandments and live in God's ways.

PRAYER. *May I abide in You, Holy Spirit, expressing my faith in word and deed.*

N wisdom one finds a spirit that is intelligent, *holy,* unique, manifold, subtle, agile, clear, unstained, certain, etc.

—Wis 7:22-23

JULY 19

REFLECTION. The Book of Wisdom speaks of the twenty-one attributes of wisdom. Seven is the perfect number in the Bible, and one forms the superlative degree by saying of the same thing three times (e.g. holy, holy, holy).

The Holy Spirit, Who is the source of all wisdom, is most perfect.

PRAYER. *Bestow Your many gifts on us, O Spirit of God, and fill us with Your wisdom.*

HE Spirit clearly says that during the last times some will abandon the faith. They will run after deceitful spirits and demonic doctrines . . . —1 Tim 4:1

JULY 20

REFLECTION. Not every new idea or theory comes from God. Many of them are the result of self-centered thinking or idle speculation.

We pray that the Spirit inform our hearts even as we listen to the teaching of the Magisterium so that we may always live in the truth.

PRAYER. *Holy Spirit, I pray for all those who have been deceived by the latest fads. Guide them home to Your truth.*

OUR gospel came to you not merely in words alone but also in power and in the Holy Spirit and with profound conviction. **—1 Thes 1:5**

JULY 21

REFLECTION. St. Paul and his companions had been beaten up before they arrived in Thessalonica. Normally, this sort of treatment would produce fear and reticence. But the Holy Spirit filled the disciples with courage.

At the same time, the Spirit moved the Thessalonians to listen to the disciples and to convert to the Lord.

PRAYER. *Spirit of God, grant me Your power and authority so that I may share Your message without fear.*

YOU are truly beautiful, my beloved. Oh, you are beautiful, your eyes are like doves. **—Song 1:15**

JULY 22

REFLECTION. The Holy Spirit is the love between the Father and the Son and Their love for us.

In Old Testament times, the dove was not a symbol of peace as it is today, it was a symbol of love. This is why the Holy Spirit appears in the form of a dove.

PRAYER. *Descend O Dove, O Spirit of love, upon Your Church and upon me.*

WE are the circumcision, we who worship by the Spirit of God and who boast in Christ Jesus and do not place any confidence in the flesh. —Phil 3:3

JULY 23

REFLECTION. Paul was fighting those who were wedded to what he considered to be archaic practices such as circumcision, dietary laws, etc. He argues that we are a new chosen people by our faith in Jesus which the Spirit has breathed into our hearts.

What we do externally should always be motivated by an internal expression of faith.

PRAYER. *Lord, let my every hope, my deepest faith be in Jesus, through the gift of faith given by the Holy Spirit.*

TO each of us, the manifestation of the Spirit is given for the common good. —1 Cor 12:7

JULY 24

REFLECTION. When the Spirit gives us various gifts, it is not for our own benefit. The Spirit does not want us to become arrogant or possessive. We are given gifts so that we might use them for the common good: the building up of the body of Christ.

This is why we should rejoice in the gifts others have received, for they are really given to all of us.

PRAYER. *Thank You, Generous Spirit, for the gifts You have given to me and to those around me.*

JOHN answered, telling them all: "I baptize you with water, but there is one coming . . . He will baptize you with the Holy Spirit and fire." **—Lk 3:16**

JULY 25

REFLECTION. John recognized that his baptism was only one of repentance, a turning away from sin. Jesus' baptism involved a turning away from sin but also being invited into the life of God through the breath of the Holy Spirit in our hearts.

The fire of the Holy Spirit will purify our hearts and inflame our love.

PRAYER. *Holy Spirit, Sanctifier, baptize me again in Your fire of love.*

IT had been revealed to him [Simeon] by the Holy Spirit that he would not experience death before he had seen the Christ of the Lord. **—Lk 2:26**

JULY 26

REFLECTION. We do not know whether Simeon received a vision or simply knew in his heart that he would see the Messiah. The Holy Spirit reveals things in many different ways (through visions, dreams, a hunger in one's heart, etc.)

The promise made to Simeon is also ours: Jesus will reveal Himself to us.

PRAYER. *Reveal Your truths, to me, O Spirit of Wisdom, and teach me how to share those insights with others.*

Y son, embrace discipline from your youth, then you will find wisdom when your hair is gray.

—Sir 6:18

JULY 27

REFLECTION. Discipline is not a dirty word. It is a spiritual tool to help us say "yes" to things that lead us to God and "no" to those things that might lead us astray.

Rather than making us self-righteous and self-absorbed, discipline helps us to have generosity of spirit.

PRAYER. *Correct me when I stray, O Spirit of Discipline, and grant me the strength I need to choose to live in Your ways.*

HO has directed the Spirit of the Lord, or Who has instructed Him as a counselor?

—Isa 40:13

JULY 28

REFLECTION. It is absurd for us to think that we can force God to do anything. God is in charge.

Yet, Jesus also taught that we are God's friends and co-workers. He answers our prayers like a loving parent who only wants what is good for His children.

PRAYER. *Thank You, God, for the incredible dignity You have granted me.*

WILL then pour out water upon the thirsty ground as well as streams upon the dry land. —Isa 44:3a

JULY 29

REFLECTION. Water is a symbol of the Holy Spirit. God promises that He will pour out that Spirit abundantly upon His people so that their faith life will become ever more fruitful.

Today we sometimes speak about going through a dry patch in our spiritual lives when it seems as if we are stuck in the desert. God turns the desert of our hearts into fertile land.

PRAYER. *Quench the thirst of my heart, O God, and refresh me in Your love.*

E not impatient when you pray and never neglect giving alms. —Sir 7:10

JULY 30

REFLECTION. There is a difference between God's time and our time. Our time passes one minute after the other. God's time is when God wills things to happen, the appointed time.

The Spirit invites us to wait patiently for the answer to our prayers for prayer is an act of surrender to God's will.

PRAYER. *Lord, teach me when to sit still and when to be active.*

HE fruit of the Spirit is . . . *self control.* There is no law against such things.

—Gal 5:22-23

JULY 31

REFLECTION. The Spirit helps us to discipline ourselves so that we can embrace that which makes us more godlike and we can reject those things that would lead us astray.

Saying "no" to certain things does not limit our freedom. Quite the opposite, we are most free when we can control our passions.

PRAYER. *Teach me patience and self-control, O Virtuous Spirit, especially when I am tempted toward anger and excess.*

O you not realize that you are God's temple, and that the Spirit of God dwells in you?

—1 Cor 3:16

AUG. 1

REFLECTION. In the Old Testament, the Jewish people had a temple in Jerusalem which was considered to be the dwelling place of God upon the earth. In the New Testament, our bodies are that temple for the Spirit of God dwells in our hearts.

As the Eucharist is bread that the Spirit makes into the body of Christ, so our bodies are Spirit-filled flesh which forms part of the Mystical body of Christ.

PRAYER. *Dwell in my heart, O Spirit of God, and consecrate me in Your grace.*

HEN the Advocate comes Whom I will send you from the Father, the Spirit of truth Who comes from the Father, He will testify on My behalf.
—Jn 15:26

AUG. 2

REFLECTION. In the Gospel of John, the Father and the Son send the Holy Spirit into the world. In the other Gospels, it is the Father and the Holy Spirit who bring Jesus into this world.

These differences are not really contradictions. We are speaking about great mysteries and there are many ways to express these ideas.

PRAYER. *May I never allow the mysteries of the faith to become obstacles to my belief.*

Y this the Holy Spirit reveals to us that as long as the first tabernacle remains standing, the way into the sanctuary has not been disclosed. **—Heb 9:8**

AUG. 3

REFLECTION. Our churches, while they are holy places, are only a foreshadowing of the glory that awaits us in heaven.

The Spirit already gives us this foretaste of what is to come, but also encourages us to long for our true home in heaven.

PRAYER. *Let me encounter You in my parish church, Lord, but let that only be the beginning.*

FTER saying this, He breathed on them and said, "Receive the Holy Spirit. If you forgive anyone's sins, they are forgiven . . ." —Jn 20:22-23

AUG. 4

REFLECTION. The sacrament of reconciliation is an encounter with the mercy of God. Sin has wounded us; it has left our hearts broken. The Holy Spirit, the love of God, heals our hearts.

The Spirit, in a sense, recreates us every time we receive forgiveness for our sins.

PRAYER. *I confess to almighty God . . .*

HE Lord God formed the first man from clay and He breathed the breath of life into his nostrils and the man became a living human being. —Gen 2:7

AUG. 5

REFLECTION. The Jewish people believed that creatures needed two things to be considered to be alive: blood and breath. Blood signifies life. Breath signifies participation in the life of the Spirit of God.

Human beings are not just fancy animals. We share in God's life.

PRAYER. *Life-giving Spirit of God, enliven me with Your breath, fill me with Your life.*

ALL of us are being transformed into that same image from glory to glory, which comes from the Lord, Who is the Spirit. **—2 Cor 3:18**

AUG. 6

REFLECTION. The Spirit already reveals the glory of God to us in those moments when we transcend our daily life and catch a glimpse of the grandeur and holiness of God. These moments, like the Transfiguration for the Apostles, give us the strength to walk the sometimes difficult path of daily life.

Have I ever caught a glimpse of the holiness of God?

PRAYER. *Unfold the veil for a moment, Lord, and let me see Your glory.*

THE Word of God is living and active. Sharper than any two-edged sword, it pierces to the point where it divides soul and spirit . . . **—Heb 4:12ab**

AUG. 7

REFLECTION. There is something about listening to or reading God's Word that reaches the inmost hidden core of our being. Even if we read it carelessly, it has a way of planting itself in our minds and hearts, and when it is the proper time, it proves to be effective.

Have I ever felt the Word of God cut away my indifference and confusion?

PRAYER. *Speak to me, O Word of God, and teach me the mysteries of Your revelation.*

N wisdom there is a spirit that *loves the good* and is keen and unhampered . . .
—Wis 7:22

AUG. 8

REFLECTION. It can, at times, be difficult to sort out what is good from what is bad, and even more difficult to sort out what is good from what is better.

It is the Holy Spirit Who provides the measure for us, telling us in our hearts what is really God's way and what falls short.

PRAYER. *Holy Spirit, grant me the wisdom to discern the good and the courage to choose it unreservedly.*

ECAUSE of His mercy, He saved me through the bath of rebirth and renewal by the Holy Spirit. **—Tit 3:5**

AUG. 9

REFLECTION. St. Paul knew very well that he didn't deserve to be called a special friend of God. He had persecuted the Church, trying to kill God's holy ones.

And yet God chose him and consecrated him to be a special instrument of God's mercy. He was more effective for the very fact that he was a concrete example of that mercy in action.

PRAYER. *May my faith life be an example of grace to those around me.*

NYONE who is victorious will be dressed like these in white robes.

—Rev 3:5a

AUG. 10

REFLECTION. Today white signifies purity. In the New Testament, white signified the power of the resurrection. (This is why the Angels in the tomb and the risen Jesus are pictured as being vested in white.)

If we conquer the way that Jesus did (by dying on the Cross), then we will share in His resurrection.

PRAYER. *Spirit of God, dress me in the white that signifies that I am one with the risen Christ.*

HE fruit of the Spirit is *love*, joy, peace, patience, kindness, generosity . . .

—Gal 5:22

AUG. 11

REFLECTION. True love is a willingness to live and even die for one another. It is not a feeling or an emotion. True love is a choice that will ultimately bring one to the Cross.

None of us has the strength to do this on our own. It is the Spirit who gives us the grace we need.

PRAYER. *Spirit of Love, teach me the true meaning of love.*

N the one Spirit we were all baptized into one body, Jews as well as Greeks, slaves as well as free men . . . —1 Cor 12:13

AUG. 12

REFLECTION. Here on earth, racial or economic distinctions are sometimes considered to be important. The Spirit reminds us that these things are insignificant in the light of our salvation.

We are all loved by God, and no matter who we are or what we do, we can all respond to that call and share in God's bounty.

PRAYER. *Spirit of Truth, help me to see our earthly distinctions for what they are.*

UT as to myself, I am filled . . . with the Spirit of the Lord . . . so that I might declare Jacob's crimes and Israel's sins to them. —Mic 3:8b

AUG. 13

REFLECTION. The Spirit of God helps us to be honest about our sinfulness.

The Spirit, the love and compassion of God, wants us to experience God's healing. Yet, we can only be healed if we admit that we need that healing, that we are broken and sinful.

PRAYER. *Spirit of God, teach me to be honest with You and myself every time I examine my conscience.*

LESSED be the God and Father of our Lord Jesus Christ Who has blessed us in Christ with every spiritual blessing in the heavens. —Eph 1:3

AUG. 14

REFLECTION. When we reflect upon the many gifts that we have received from the Holy Spirit, our only possible response is gratitude. These gifts include our talents and holy desires, etc.

There are even gifts that we have not yet discerned but which will make themselves evident in God's time.

PRAYER. *Help me to discern Your gifts to me, O Holy Gift of God, and teach me to use them well.*

WAS caught up in the spirit, and there in heaven I beheld a throne. —Rev 4:2

AUG. 15

REFLECTION. We do not know whether this visionary is saying that he experienced a vision or was physically carried up to heaven. Either way, he stood before the throne of God.

The Blessed Virgin Mary, when her life on earth was complete, was transported by the Spirit body and soul into heaven.

PRAYER. *Fill me with Your Spirit, Lord, as You did the Blessed Virgin Mary, so that I may know Your glory.*

HEN he said to me, "Do not seal up the words of prophecy that are in this book, for the time is near."

—Rev 22:10

AUG. 16

REFLECTION. Normally, those who received apocalyptic visions were told to seal up their books until the time was ready. But the death and resurrection of Jesus already began the end times.

Now is the time to turn our hearts over to the Lord. We don't know how much time we have until we are called home.

PRAYER. *May I use each moment, O Spirit of the Prophets, as if it were a precious gift from You.*

SPIRIT of *strength* and a spirit of knowledge and of fear of the Lord . . .

—Isa 11:2

AUG. 17

REFLECTION. Strength does not mean that we can overpower others. Sometimes the strongest person is the one who can be vulnerable.

Strength means being able to do what is right and good. It means not being swept away by what is popular or convenient.

PRAYER. *Make me strong, O Spirit of God, even when this means I must admit that I am weak.*

WHILE Jesus was engaged in prayer after also having been baptized, heaven opened and the Holy Spirit descended on Him in bodily form like a dove. —Lk 3:21-22

AUG. 18

REFLECTION. While Jesus prays occasionally in the Gospels of Matthew and Mark, He prays frequently in the Gospel of Luke. He prays to discern the Father's will and to have the courage to embrace it.

When we allow the Spirit to guide our prayers, then we, too, know what God wants of us and we are able to say yes to that call.

PRAYER. *What do You want of me, Lord? Send Your Spirit into my heart to inform me.*

EACH of the four living creatures had six wings, and all of them were covered with eyes all around and underneath their wings. —Rev 4:8

AUG. 19

REFLECTION. The four living creatures represent the best of creation. The lion is the king of the beasts, the ox the king of farm animals, the eagle the king of birds and the human the king of all creation.

The eyes on their wings represent the presence of the Holy Spirit, for creation reveals the goodness and grandeur of God to us.

PRAYER. *May I see Your creative presence in all that I see around me.*

N wisdom there is a spirit that is *holy,* unique and yet manifold . . .

—Wis 7:22

AUG. 20

REFLECTION. In the Bible, the word "holy" means to be totally other, someone or something that is so beyond our comprehension that it fills us with a sense of awe and wonder.

As we experience the action of the Holy Spirit in our lives, we are filled with that awe for God's ways are so far beyond ours.

PRAYER. *Fill my heart with wonder, O Glorious Spirit of God.*

EEP watch over yourselves and over all the flock of which the Holy Spirit has made you overseers . . .

—Acts 20:28

AUG. 21

REFLECTION. We believe that the Spirit of God guides the choice of our Holy Father and also guides him in his ministry of leading the Church.

Still, he is human and needs our prayers each day to be able to fulfill his enormous responsibilities.

PRAYER. *Lord, bless and protect our Holy Father and our bishops.*

ND to such a person I will also give the morning star.

—Rev 2:28

AUG. 22

REFLECTION. Jesus rose from the dead just before dawn on Easter Sunday. The morning star, Venus, rises just before the dawn. Venus was considered to be the goddess of love and victory. Love conquered death early on Easter morning.

Jesus shares that gift with those who are willing to die with Him so that they might rise with Him.

PRAYER. *Raise me up from the death of sin, O Spirit of Life, and raise me up from the sleep of death on the last day.*

HEN the Spirit of truth comes, He will guide you into all the truth.

—Jn 16:13

AUG. 23

REFLECTION. There were so many wrong decisions that the early Church could have made, so many ways that it could have fallen into error. Yet, the Spirit guided it along the right path.

If we only open our minds and hearts to the Spirit's guidance, then we, too, will never lose our way.

PRAYER. *Spirit of Truth, reveal Your truth to me.*

HERE appeared to them tongues as of fire which separated and came to rest on each one of them.

—Acts 2:3

AUG. 24

REFLECTION. When the Apostles and the Blessed Virgin Mary received the Holy Spirit on Pentecost Sunday, each of them received an individual flame over their heads. This is a reminder that each of us receives that gift which is most appropriate to us.

The gift of the Spirit is not generic. It is personal and intimate.

PRAYER. *Consuming Fire, grant me those gifts which You judge to be best for me.*

N the last and greatest day of the feast, Jesus stood up and cried out, "If anyone is thirsty, let him come to Me and drink." —Jn 7:37

AUG. 25

REFLECTION. One of the symbols of the Feast of Dedication was water. Jesus explains that He is the source of living water. That water represents the Spirit of God flowing into our hearts.

Jesus and the Father pour that Spirit upon us and the Spirit quenches the deepest thirst of our hearts.

PRAYER. *Source of heavenly water, quench the desert-like thirst of my soul.*

HEN Simon saw that the Spirit was bestowed by the laying on of the Apostles' hands, he offered them money. —Acts 8:18

AUG. 26

REFLECTION. Simon misinterpreted the action of the Holy Spirit as being a form of magic. The Spirit works through love, not magic.

Prayer should likewise be an act of love in which we trust that God will give us the most loving answer possible and not magic in which we try to control God.

PRAYER. *May I never allow my forms of piety to become acts of superstition or magic.*

HE fruit of the Spirit is *patience*, kindness, generosity and faithfulness . . . —Gal 5:22-23

AUG. 27

REFLECTION. Things are not always done by our schedules. There are two words in the Bible for time. One simply means one minute after another (*kronos*). The other (*kairos*) means God's appointed time.

We often have to wait for God to unfold His plan in His time. We are not in charge.

PRAYER. *Lord, may I be patient with You, with others, and even with myself.*

O they fell prostrate and cried, "God of spirits and all humanity, will one person's sin make You angry with all of us?"

—Num 16:22

AUG. 28

REFLECTION. The ancients recognized that there was both a spiritual and physical world. We sometimes get so caught up with the material world that we lose track of that other dimension of reality.

The Holy Spirit keeps reminding us that there are levels of reality that cannot be measured but which are nevertheless real.

PRAYER. *I believe in God Who created the visible and the invisible.*

UST as the body is dead without a spirit, so faith without works is also dead.

—Jas 2:26

AUG. 29

REFLECTION. It is the Spirit of God breathed into us when we were conceived which gave us life (both physical and spiritual life). Life in God has to be expressed both by what we believe and what we do.

Without faith, we are all but dead.

PRAYER. *Holy Spirit, breathe Your life into my heart and my actions.*

HE LORD bestowed the Spirit on the seventy elders and they prophesied as the Spirit came to rest on them.

—Num 11:25

AUG. 30

REFLECTION. The Spirit of God guided Moses in his decision to seek assistance from the elders of Israel.

We are called to discern God's will, fulfill that will, and even after we have finished doing what we are doing, examine what we did to make sure that it was God's will.

PRAYER. *Guide me, Spirit of God, along Your ways.*

HE spirits of the Prophets are subject to their Prophets' control . . .

—1 Cor 14:32

AUG. 31

REFLECTION. Prophets in the early Christian community interpreted the Sacred Scripture and then applied its lessons to daily life. Today we would call this preaching.

This had to be intelligible if the community was to benefit, so the Prophets in the community needed both enthusiasm and reason.

PRAYER. *Guide those who preach in my parish, O Holy Spirit, so that they may express Your truth well and with enthusiasm.*

[PROPHETS] were searching out the time and the circumstances to which the Spirit of Christ within them was pointing when it testified to the sufferings that Christ would endure . . . —1 Pet 1:11

SEPT. 1

REFLECTION. The Jewish people expected their Messiah to be triumphant. Yet, some of the Prophets also spoke of the Messiah's sufferings.

They would not have thought of this on their own. It was only through the inspiration of the Holy Spirit that they could have foretold such an incredible development.

PRAYER. *Let me understand that which does not make sense and embrace that which is beyond my comprehension.*

NOW Joshua, the son of Nun, was filled with the Spirit of Wisdom for Moses had laid his hands upon him. —Deut 34:9

SEPT. 2

REFLECTION. Moses recognized that he had reached the end of his life, so he imposed his hands upon Joshua, his successor. He did not try to hold on to this responsibility as if it were his own possession.

Wisdom calls us to know when to pass on our authority and responsibilities to someone who can do it better.

PRAYER. *Lord, let me serve You and the community as long as You desire.*

NYONE who is victorious I will make into a pillar in the temple of my God, and never again will he depart from it. —Rev 3:12

SEPT. 3

REFLECTION. Life is filled with insecurity. We sometimes wonder whether there is anything that will last forever.

God's fidelity will never be shaken. We will be like a stable pillar in God's house.

PRAYER. *Make my faith firm and unshakable, O Spirit of Fortitude, so that I may always dwell in You.*

ISDOM that comes from above is . . . without any trace of partiality or hypocrisy. —Jas 3:17

SEPT. 4

REFLECTION. It is so easy to buy into the false judgments that many people make of each other. We hear lies and exaggerations. The Spirit of Wisdom helps us to discover what the real truth is.

What causes divisions and harmful disagreements in my faith community?

PRAYER. *Spirit of Truth, let me see others as You see them.*

S anyone among you sick? He should send for the presbyters of the Church so that they may pray over him and anoint him with oil . . . —Jas 5:14

SEPT. 5

REFLECTION. The Spirit of God is the source of all healing, both physical and spiritual. We pray that whatever is broken in us might be healed, but we also do our part (e.g. going to the doctor, eating right, going to a counselor).

God works both directly and through intermediaries.

PRAYER. *I pray for all of those who will receive the Sacrament of Anointing today. Bless them and heal them in Your love.*

HERE was a man in Jerusalem whose name was Simeon. This upright and devout man . . . the Holy Spirit rested upon him. —Lk 2:25

SEPT. 6

REFLECTION. Simeon was a man of prayer, and so he was open to the promptings of the Spirit. Thus, when the Holy Family entered the temple, Simeon could sense their presence and the fact that Jesus, their Child, was the One for Whom he had prayed.

When we are people of prayer, we are likewise open to the Spirit's promptings.

PRAYER. *Lord, my eyes have seen the salvation which You have prepared in the sight of all the nations.*

E speak of these things in words taught to us not by human wisdom but by the Spirit, expressing spiritual things in spiritual words.

—1 Cor 2:13

SEPT. 7

REFLECTION. Science and other forms of human knowledge can lead us only so far when we speak about spiritual things. God's ways are mysterious and beyond our understanding.

Yet, through revelation, we do have spiritual words and concepts that can lead us in the right direction in order to delve into the mysteries of our faith.

PRAYER. *May my thoughts be spiritual, Holy Spirit of God, and not mired in what is worldly.*

IVE evidence of Your deeds of old, and fulfill the prophecies that have been spoken in Your name.

—Sir 36:14

SEPT. 8

REFLECTION. The Holy Spirit inspired the Prophets to speak in God's name. That same Holy Spirit also moves in our history (of God's people and of our own lives) so that these prophecies might be fulfilled.

This reminds us that God has a plan for us: that we be saved and live in His love for all eternity.

PRAYER. *May I be as ready to embrace Your plan, O Spirit of God, as was the Blessed Virgin Mary.*

THE Spirit of the Lord has come upon me because the Lord has anointed me . . . to proclaim liberty to captives . . .

—Isa 61:1

SEPT. 9

REFLECTION. The Spirit led St. Peter Claver to work among the slaves being brought from Africa to the New World. Unlike most of those who dealt with them, Peter treated them with love and compassion.

Do I treat everyone I encounter with sacred respect?

PRAYER. *Let me see You, O God, in the faces of those who are suffering.*

DID you receive the Spirit by observing the Law or by believing what you heard?

—Gal 3:2

SEPT. 10

REFLECTION. Our faith is a gift from God through the Holy Spirit and not something that we earn.

When we do good deeds, God does not love us more. What changes is that we are more able to accept that free gift of love with which God already loves us.

PRAYER. *O Gracious Gift of God, fill me with gratitude for the incredible generosity You have shown me.*

OR if the Gentiles have come to share in their spiritual blessings, they owe it to them to share their material blessings with them. **—Rom 15:27**

SEPT. 11

REFLECTION. Our faith has two dimensions: vertical and horizontal. The vertical dimension involves our relationship with God. We are truly blessed when God is part of our lives. But our faith also has a horizontal dimension: the willingness to serve others.

God has blessed us so that we might be able to share our bounty with those who are in need.

PRAYER. *May I love You, God, and love my neighbor as myself.*

HE Spirit explores everything, even the depths of God. **—1 Cor 2:10**

SEPT. 12

REFLECTION. Because the Holy Spirit is a totally spiritual entity, the Spirit both knows the very profound mysteries of Who God is and is able to reveal this mystery to us.

St. Paul compares it to how our soul knows the most profound dimension of who we are.

PRAYER. *Spirit of God, reveal the mysteries of Who You are to me.*

N wisdom there is a *clear* spirit that is unstained and certain . . .

—Wis 7:22

SEPT. 13

REFLECTION. As we discern God's will in our lives, we often realize that there are layers of mixed motives in our hearts. The Holy Spirit, on the other hand, has only one transparent motive: to bring us to God.

The more we allow the Spirit to clarify the motives of our hearts, the more we are able to respond generously to God's call.

PRAYER. *Look into my heart, Holy Spirit, and clarify anything that is muddled and confused.*

ESIRES of the flesh result in death, but desires of the spirit result in life and peace.

—Rom 8:6

SEPT. 14

REFLECTION. We can only find peace when we are willing to root out of our lives those things which have become a distraction to us: our passions, material goods, etc.

We cannot hope to be fully alive until we are willing to die to ourselves so that we might live in Christ.

PRAYER. *Sanctifying Spirit of God, teach me to discipline the desires of my flesh.*

THE Spirit of the Lord is upon me, because the Lord has anointed me . . . to comfort all those who mourn.

—Isa 61:1-2

SEPT. 15

REFLECTION. The Blessed Virgin Mary shared the sufferings of her Son, just as all loving parents experience the pain of their children.

The Holy Spirit provides consolation for all who mourn. The Spirit is the source of our hope that one day love will conquer death and pain and sin.

PRAYER. *O Lady of Sorrows, pray for us.*

ANYONE who is victorious . . . I will give authority over the nations, the same authority that I received from my Father.

—Rev 2:26-27

SEPT. 16

REFLECTION. We are victors when we die with Christ so that we may live with Him.

Even though dying to ourselves may sound as if we are "losing," we have actually conquered the forces of hate and division by choosing to love even unto death.

PRAYER. *Teach me, O Spirit of God, to judge my success not by how much I acquire but rather by how much I have loved.*

WILL pray with the spirit, but I will also pray with my mind.

—1 Cor 14:15

SEPT. 17

REFLECTION. The community in Corinth thought that speaking in tongues was the most important gift because one was allowing the Spirit to take possession of one's consciousness. Paul argues that teaching in an intelligible way was more important for it helped build up the community.

Are my prayers expressions of my intellect, my emotion, my hopes and even my fears?

PRAYER. *May I pray in body, soul, and spirit.*

HEN He [the Paraclete] comes, He will prove the world wrong about sin and righteousness and judgment.

—Jn 16:8

SEPT. 18

REFLECTION. The Spirit has not only come into the world to offer consolation. The Spirit has also come to let us know when we have chosen the wrong path. We humans can easily rationalize our actions and fool ourselves concerning what we are doing.

The Spirit helps us to sort out our self-delusions and to choose the right path.

PRAYER. *O Spirit of Truth, challenge and correct me when that will bring me closer to You.*

OWEVER, if by the Spirit you put to death the deeds of the body, you will live. —Rom 8:13

SEPT. 19

REFLECTION. We communicate what we're really about by the way we live our lives. If we are concerned with our comfort and amusement, then we will be shallow. If we are consumed by anger and resentment, people will realize that something is wrong.

But if we dedicate ourselves to prayer and study and compassion, people will sense that we are one with God.

PRAYER. *Lord, may I only and always live for and in Your Spirit.*

HE Church throughout Judea, Galilee and Samaria enjoyed peace, building up strength and living in the fear of the Lord. —Acts 9:31

SEPT. 20

REFLECTION. It is so easy to feel responsible for others' faith lives, as if we could control what our spouses or children or friends think. We have to remember that it is the Holy Spirit Who gives the gift of faith and causes that gift to grow in people's hearts.

But God works in God's time and not ours.

PRAYER. *Author of all Good, may I and my family grow stronger in our faith.*

NYONE who is victorious . . . I will inscribe on him the name of my God and the name of the city of my God. **—Rev 3:12**

SEPT. 21

REFLECTION. To the Jewish mind, names are very important. They do more than just identify a person. They somehow give one power and authority over that person.

If we have God's name and the name of the holy city written upon us, then we have been given a new identity. We become the temple in which He dwells. We become holy ground.

PRAYER. *Spirit of God, engrave Your name upon my heart.*

HEN their sinfulness grew more and more . . . there appeared a Prophet [Elijah] whose words were like a fiery furnace. **—Sir 47:24-48:1**

SEPT. 22

REFLECTION. The Holy Spirit is often associated with fire. At times, fire is positive, e.g. the fire that lights a way or warms those who are cold.

In the case of Elijah, it was a castigating fire that would burn away the impurity of the people of Israel. Being forceful like Elijah is sometimes the appropriate response to a situation that has gotten out of hand.

PRAYER. *Spirit of Purity, burn away that which is impure in my heart.*

HILE Peter was still speaking, the Holy Spirit descended upon all who were listening to his message. **—Acts 10:44**

SEPT. 23

REFLECTION. St. Peter was guided in his actions by the Holy Spirit. He needed the Spirit's guidance to lead the Church along the right way.

All throughout the Acts of the Apostles, we hear how the Spirit guided the actions of the disciples, e.g., how they should live, where they should preach, etc.

PRAYER. *Holy Spirit, govern Your Church with Your gifts of wisdom and love.*

ESTORE to me the joy of being saved, and grant me the strength of a generous spirit. **—Ps 51:14**

SEPT. 24

REFLECTION. There are times when we know what we should do but we just don't have the courage to do it. The Holy Spirit gives us the strength to choose the right path and to pursue it no matter what the cost is.

While we can't always do the right thing on our own, God can do it in and through us.

PRAYER. *Spirit of God, may I always seek Your help.*

END forth wisdom from Your holy heavens and from Your glorious throne dispatch her. —Wis 9:10a

SEPT. 25

REFLECTION. In Old Testament times, people began to speak about God as if He lived at the other end of the universe and had nothing to do with us. But God showers His Spirit of wisdom upon us so that we can know and love Him.

Even if God is filled with mystery, He is not hidden for He has revealed Himself to us.

PRAYER. *Spirit of God, make known to me Who You are and what You want of me.*

HE lion roars—who would not fear? The Lord God speaks—who would not prophesy? —Am 3:8

SEPT. 26

REFLECTION. Amos was not a professional Prophet, but once the Spirit called him, he found that he could not do anything else. It was as automatic with him as it is to be frightened when one encounters a roaring lion.

When the Spirit speaks to us, we really don't have a choice. If we want to be authentic, people of the truth, we have to obey.

PRAYER. *Spirit of God, roar Your truth into my ears and my heart.*

E have not received the spirit of the world but the Spirit Who is from God, so that we may understand the gifts bestowed upon us by God.

—1 Cor 2:12

SEPT. 27

REFLECTION. The Spirit of the world offers easy and comfortable answers to our difficulties. The Spirit of God challenges us to be God-like: generous, merciful, kind, virtuous, etc.

Those who live by the values of the world will not understand these things, but spiritual people will.

PRAYER. *Generous Spirit of God, root out from my heart anything that is worldly and unworthy of grace.*

E [The Spirit] will glorify Me, for He will take what is Mine and communicate it to you. —Jn 16:14

SEPT. 28

REFLECTION. When we speak about how the persons of the Trinity interact, the Father, the Son, and the Holy Spirit, we see tremendous generosity and service and love. None of Them try to hold onto Their glory. Their only desire is to share it with others.

Their goal is not to possess, it is to give and serve.

PRAYER. *Holy Spirit, teach me the generosity of the Trinity so that I may give of myself to You and to my neighbors.*

THEN the Angel showed me the river of the water of life, bright as crystal, flowing from the throne of God and of the Lamb . . . —Rev 22:1

SEPT. 29

REFLECTION. The river of water is the grace of God given to us through the Holy Spirit. Angels try to lead us to that grace by teaching us to surrender our will to that of God.

We sometimes picture Angels as cute and gentle. They are also powerful messengers who call us to worship our God and serve our neighbor.

PRAYER. *Angel of God, protecting Spirit of God, guide my soul to Your life and Your truth.*

ALL Scripture is inspired by God and is useful for teaching, for refutation, for correction, and for training in uprightness. . . . —2 Tim 3:16

SEPT. 30

REFLECTION. The Holy Spirit inspired the authors of the books of the Bible, uniting the divine breath with their human talents, producing the living Word of God.

We call upon the Holy Spirit to inspire our reading and study of Holy Scripture so that we, too, may encounter the living word of God.

PRAYER. *Holy Spirit, inspire my efforts as I read and meditate upon Holy Scripture.*

AY the God of hope fill you with all joy and peace in believing, so that you may grow rich in hope by the power of the Holy Spirit.

—Rom 15:13

OCT. 1

REFLECTION. The Spirit of God gave St. Therese a childlike simplicity which speaks to so many.

Yet, she is considered to be a Doctor of the Church for her simple insights are actually powerfully profound. She taught that very few of us will do great things, but all of us can do things with great love.

PRAYER. *St. Therese, teach me to do small things with great love.*

HEN You send forth Your Spirit, they are created, and You renew the face of the earth.

—Ps 104:30

OCT. 2

REFLECTION. God created the world through the action of His Spirit. God can recreate it in His image through His Spirit.

We pray that the Spirit of God will help us to transform this created world into the Kingdom of God, a place where all of the goods of this world lead us to holiness and not into temptation.

PRAYER. *Breathe forth Your Spirit upon us and the world, God, and renew us all in Your image.*

N previous times, God spoke to our ancestors in many and various ways through the Prophets . . . —Heb 1:1

OCT. 3

REFLECTION. The Holy Spirit speaks to us even as the Spirit spoke through the Prophets, but they and we often filter that message through our own needs and wants. This is why Jesus had to come into the world: to teach us clearly Who God is and what God wants of us.

We ask the Spirit to open our ears and minds to Jesus' message.

PRAYER. *Speak to my heart, O Spirit of God, and reveal Your truths to my mind.*

HE fruit of the Spirit is . . . *peace*, patience, kindness, generosity, faithfulness . . . —Gal 5:22

OCT. 4

REFLECTION. When we surrender to God's will, we are filled with a profound peace because we trust that God will be with us no matter what happens. The Spirit teaches us to let go of control: to let go and to let God.

Am I a peace-filled person?

PRAYER. *Lord, make me an instrument of Your peace.*

HERE are three witnesses: the Spirit, the water and the blood, and these three are as one. —1 Jn 5:7-8

OCT. 5

REFLECTION. The Holy Spirit testifies in our heart to the truth of Jesus' message. We also have external proof in the water and the blood. The water stands for the Sacrament of Baptism. The blood stands for the Sacrament of the Eucharist.

Thus, our faith is affirmed both internally and externally.

PRAYER. *May I hear and live in Your truth, both inside and out.*

HEN the Spirit is poured on us from on high . . . righteousness will dwell in the desert and justice will abide in the orchard.—Isa 32:15-16

OCT. 6

REFLECTION. When we open our hearts to the action of the Holy Spirit, we are filled with God's wisdom and righteousness. This helps us to live a good life—treating other people with great respect, forgiving those who have hurt us, giving them good example, etc.

What relationships in my life need the Spirit's healing?

PRAYER. *Heal my heart, Holy Spirit, and mend the broken relationships that weigh upon me.*

BRETHREN, I exhort you by Our Lord Jesus Christ and by the love of the Spirit, to join me in my labors by praying to God for me. **—Rom 15:30**

OCT. 7

REFLECTION. When we pray, we join our love to that of God's, and that love embraces the person for whom we are praying. And love always has an effect for it heals us spiritually and physically. It gives us insight and courage and peace.

When we accompany others with our prayers, we are giving them the most precious gift we could ever give.

PRAYER. *Lord, I lift up . . . . to You today. Bring healing and comfort into his/her life.*

IF you then . . . know how to give good gifts to your children, how much more will Your heavenly Father give the Holy Spirit to those who ask Him! **—Lk 11:13**

OCT. 8

REFLECTION. God the Father wants to give us the gift of the Holy Spirit. He wants us to share in His eternal life. But our hearts have to be open to receive that gift.

God cannot force His love upon us. He can only offer it in the hope that we will embrace what He offers.

PRAYER. *Holy Spirit, open the door of my heart to receive You into my life.*

THIS same anointing teaches you everything, and is true and not false, so abide in Him just as He taught you.
—1 Jn 2:27b

OCT. 9

REFLECTION. How do we decide what is true or false? Ultimately, it is not based upon our desires or what the majority of people think. The truth is not relative or changeable.

There is no falsity or ambiguity in God's Spirit (whether we are speaking about moral truth or theological truth or the deepest truths of love and goodness).

PRAYER. *Teach me Your truth, O Spirit of God, and guide my actions in Your ways.*

WHAT is born of flesh is flesh, and what is born of the Spirit is spirit.
—Jn 3:6

OCT. 10

REFLECTION. Typical of the Gospel of John, this passage shows a strong dualism. We are offered a choice between flesh and spirit, death and life, darkness and light, false teaching and the truth.

If we choose to live in the Spirit, it means that we must reject the things of the flesh, those things that drag us down.

PRAYER. *Let me be born again in Your Spirit, Lord.*

N His hand is the soul of every living creature as well as the life breath of all humanity.

—Job 12:10

OCT. 11

REFLECTION. Job reminds us how fragile human life is. God created us by breathing His Spirit into a lump of mud, making Adam into a living person. If God takes that breath away, then we return to dust.

This fact should not fill us with dread. It should engender gratitude for God keeps us in being every second of our lives.

PRAYER. *I thank You for the gift of life, O Lord. Let me use every moment You have given me well.*

IS delight shall be found in the *fear of the Lord* [piety].

—Isa 11:3

OCT. 12

REFLECTION. This is one of the seven gifts of the Holy Spirit. The sixth and seventh gifts are both called "fear of the Lord," but in the Greek translation of this verse is translated as piety.

When we are in the presence of the holy, we should have a spirit of reverence, a respect for the sacred.

PRAYER. *Let me be childlike in my awe and wonder, O Holy Spirit, before the mysteries of Your love.*

HOW long, O you simple ones, will you love inanity and how long will you reject my reproof? —Prov 1:22-23

OCT. 13

REFLECTION. The Holy Spirit, at times, consoles us, but at other times the Spirit challenges us. This is true love, for one does not allow those whom one loves to continue in their error without trying to bring them around.

People might not always accept our reproofs, but the Spirit impels us to be honest with them.

PRAYER. *Give me the courage, Holy Spirit, to be honest with those who have lost their way.*

THEN he brought me back to the entrance of the temple and there I saw water flowing out from beneath the threshold of the temple. —Ezek 47:1

OCT. 14

REFLECTION. The Prophet Ezekiel speaks of the river of grace that would flow from Israel's worship in the temple.

In the New Testament, we understand that river of grace as the gift of the Spirit, for the Spirit calls us to worship God and makes our worship a source of grace and blessing.

PRAYER. *May my prayers and acts of worship be authentic and sincere, O God.*

E establish plans in our hearts, but the tongues witness what is from the Lord. —Prov 16:1

OCT. 15

REFLECTION. St. Theresa recognized that her life was guided by the Spirit. She once said, "How do you make God laugh?" The answer was, "Tell Him your plans!"

By being open to the Spirit, we can discern what God wants of us and embrace it with enthusiasm.

PRAYER. *May Your will always be mine, O Lord.*

WILL pour out My spirit upon all humans . . . your young people shall see visions. —Joel 3:1

OCT. 16

REFLECTION. St. Margaret Mary was given insight into the love of God through her visions of the Sacred Heart.

It is God's Spirit which enables us to experience that love for the Spirit is the love of God which dwells in our hearts.

PRAYER. *Teach me Your lessons of love, O Spirit of God, for on my own I cannot even know what love truly means.*

OMPELLED by the Spirit, I am on my way to Jerusalem . . . in every city the Holy Spirit warns me that I face imprisonment and hardships.

—Acts 20:22-23

OCT. 17

REFLECTION. The Holy Spirit often challenges us to take up our crosses to follow Jesus. There are times that we have to recognize that it is going to get ugly and to accept it.

St. Ignatius was killed for the faith in Rome, but by giving up his life, he gave a powerful witness of love and faith.

PRAYER. *Let my life be the wheat which You grind to form the host of Your presence in the world.*

NROLLING the scroll, He found the passage where it is written, "The Spirit of the Lord is upon Me . . ."

—Lk 4:17-18

OCT. 18

REFLECTION. Luke, moved by the Spirit, speaks of how Jesus reached out in a special way to the *anawim,* the poor ones of the Lord.

They are the people who are broken and who therefore recognize their need for God to be a part of their lives.

PRAYER. *May Your Spirit move me to serve Your little ones, O Lord.*

JESUS came and proclaimed peace to you who were far away and peace to those who were near. For through Him we both have access to the Father in the one Spirit.

—Eph 2:17-18

OCT. 19

REFLECTION. It is the Spirit of God that heals the divisions among us. We see this in the story of St. Isaac Jogues who was willing to die out of love for the Native Americans.

If we live in the Spirit, we cannot afford to treat anyone as if they were our enemy for the Spirit of God abides in the hearts of all.

PRAYER. *Spirit of unity and peace, bring us all into one Church united by Your love.*

TEST everything, and hold fast to what is good. Avoid every form of evil.

—1 Thes 5:21-22

OCT. 20

REFLECTION. We cannot assume that everything we hear comes from God. Even some spiritual phenomena, e.g., the ability to heal, a "holy" demeanor, etc., can be a front or can be produced by forces that are not from God.

We must test all things and embrace what comes from God while we reject what comes from the evil one.

PRAYER. *Holy Spirit, let me not be confused by appearances. Let me discern clearly what comes from You.*

PAPHRAS, our fellow servant and faithful minister of Christ on your behalf. He was also the one who made known to us your love in the Spirit. —Col 1:7-8

OCT. 21

REFLECTION. One can determine if a person is a true Christian by the person's embrace of the truth and the willingness of the person to live in love.

Embracing the truth is an intellectual assent to our beliefs. Living in love is the emotive response to our faith. Neither of these is just a "feeling," for they are ultimately choices we make in the Lord.

PRAYER. *May I choose to live in You and Your love, O Lord.*

ND because you are sons, God has sent into our hearts the Spirit of His Son, crying out "Abba! Father!" —Gal 4:6

OCT. 22

REFLECTION. On our own, we wouldn't dare suppose that Gods love us as profoundly as a parent loves children. But there is something in our heart that longs for such a relationship.

It is the Spirit of God who tells us that we should long for it because it is the Spirit Who makes it real.

PRAYER. *May I always believe the Spirit's revelation that God is Abba.*

F one loves justice, then the fruit of her works are seen to be virtuous.

—Wis 8:7a

OCT. 23

REFLECTION. Justice and righteousness are the products of a life based on virtue. It is not enough to obey laws. We must internalize our values so that they might be witnessed by the virtues we practice.

The Spirit both reveals to us the virtues we need and gives us the ability to embrace them.

PRAYER. *Fill my life with virtue, Holy Spirit, so that my witness might be authentic and pure.*

HEY say that the Prophet is a fool, and the spiritual man is mad. Because their iniquity is great, so, too, is their hostility.

—Hos 9:7

OCT. 24

REFLECTION. We sometimes become defensive and angry when people point out our faults. Yet, if we are to grow in the Lord, we must learn to hear the truth in what they are saying (even if the way they are saying it is offensive.)

A truly spiritual person is never afraid to grow.

PRAYER. *Correct me, O Holy Spirit, through the words of others and through Your revelations in my heart.*

OU have been sanctified, you have been justified in the name of the Lord Jesus Christ and in the Spirit of God.

—1 Cor 6:11

OCT. 25

REFLECTION. To be justified means to live at peace with God. We find that peace by living in faith, by trusting in the love Jesus expressed for us on the cross.

To be sanctified means to be set apart by the Spirit so that we might serve God.

PRAYER. *Set me apart to do Your will, O Spirit of God, and let me always live in Your peace.*

F the Spirit of Him who raised Jesus from the dead dwells in you, then the one who raised Christ from the dead will also give life to your mortal bodies . . . —Rom 8:11

OCT. 26

REFLECTION. Our mortal bodies are fated to die, yet the Spirit raised Jesus' mortal body from the dead. St. Paul promises that the same Spirit will raise our bodies from the dead.

We will have a glorified body that will no longer experience the limitations of the bodies we now have.

PRAYER. *Life-giving Spirit of God, may I be so filled with Your life that even when I die, I will live with You.*

ISDOM is the image of God's goodness, and she who is one, can do all things . . .

—Wis 7:26-27

OCT. 27

REFLECTION. When the Spirit bestows the gift of wisdom upon us, we are able to understand what is truly good and what only appears to be good.

This discernment gives us the freedom to choose what is right and just in our everyday lives with the certainty that we are not deluding ourselves.

PRAYER. *Spirit of Wisdom, clarify my intentions and purify my thoughts.*

HE Spirit of Truth Who comes from the Father, He will testify on my behalf.

—Jn 15:26

OCT. 28

REFLECTION. We are co-workers with God. The Holy Spirit gives witness to our faith in our hearts, but the Holy Spirit also acts through the witness that we give in our actions.

This is an incredible dignity, to share in the Holy Spirit's mission to proclaim the Good News.

PRAYER. *Spirit of Truth, may I give witness to the Good News in my life.*

E endows us with the knowledge to be able to glory in His mighty works.

—Sir 38:6

OCT. 29

REFLECTION. The Holy Spirit teaches us that the world around us was created by God. We can see God's fingerprints in every beauty found in nature.

We praise the Lord for His majesty and wonder.

PRAYER. *Be praised, God of creation, for the wonders of Your love.*

N wisdom one finds a spirit that is not *baneful.*

—Wis 7:22

OCT. 30

REFLECTION. To be a bane is to be poisonous or dangerous, to be harmful to others. The Holy Spirit is the exact opposite of that. The Spirit heals us and comforts us and calls us to our greatest potential.

The Spirit only wants what is good for us, even when that means that the Spirit at times calls us to the Cross.

PRAYER. *Spirit of Wisdom, teach me what is truly good for me.*

HE Lord appeared to Abraham at the terebinth of Mamre. . . . He looked up and saw three men standing nearby.

—Gen 18:1-2

OCT. 31

REFLECTION. In Genesis, the three visitors were God and two Angels (the same Angels who later exacted judgment upon Sodom and Gomorrah).

In light of the New Testament, we realize that they are also symbols of the Holy Trinity: the Father, the Son and the Holy Spirit. Although we would not know about the Trinity until Jesus revealed it, it was already being revealed in mystery in Old Testament times.

PRAYER. *Glory be to the Father, and to the Son, and to the Holy Spirit. . .*

OU were marked with the seal of the Holy Spirit Who had been promised. That Spirit is the down payment of our inheritance . . .

—Eph 1:13-14

NOV. 1

REFLECTION. God has promised us that if we remain faithful, we will share in His love forever. But we do not have to wait until we arrive in heaven to live in that love.

We already experience that love here on this earth through the Spirit, and we will see the fulfillment of that love in heaven.

PRAYER. *Seal me with the Spirit of Your love, O God, so that I may be one with You.*

HUS the Lord God says to the bones: "See! I will place My Spirit within you so that you might come back to life."

—Ezek 37:5

NOV. 2

REFLECTION. Just as the Spirit of God descended upon a field of dried bones in the days of Ezekiel, so also the Holy Spirit will be breathed into us to raise us up from the dead on the day of the Lord.

God has not destined us for death but rather for life everlasting.

PRAYER. *Eternal rest grant unto them, O Lord . . .*

ND the fruit of the Spirit is . . . *gentleness*, and self-control.

—Gal 5:22-23

NOV. 3

REFLECTION. The action of the Spirit leads to peace and gentleness.

If we see others sinning, it should prompt compassion in us and not judgmentalism. If we see people in need, we should respond to their need with the gentleness of a loving parent.

PRAYER. *O Holy Spirit, give me the gift of being meek and gentle like Jesus, the Lamb of God.*

WILL pour My Spirit out upon your offspring, and My blessings upon your descendants.

—Isa 44:3b

NOV. 4

REFLECTION. When we live in the Spirit, the blessings of God are showered upon us and all those around us. People sense the change in us and the profound peace that we have found. They will want to know our secret.

Furthermore, we will be able to love them in a way that is pure and holy.

PRAYER. *May I be an instrument of healing for all those around me.*

" 

ES," says the Spirit, "they will find rest from their labors, for their deeds go with them."

—Rev 14:13

NOV. 5

REFLECTION. Our heavenly reward is a free gift from God. Jesus paid the price for our sins.

Yet, God expects us to do our part. We have to respond to God's loving gift with our good works. What we do on earth somehow continues into our afterlife in heaven.

PRAYER. *May I work as if it all depends upon me, remembering it all depends upon You.*

HEN the Lord said, "My Spirit is not going to remain in humans forever, since they are but flesh . . ." —Gen 6:3

NOV. 6

REFLECTION. God created Adam by breathing His Spirit into a lump of clay. But Adam's sin all but extinguished that Spirit and our life span became limited.

When Jesus rose from the dead, He breathed His Spirit into His disciples, giving us the gift of life that even death cannot conquer: life everlasting.

PRAYER. *Never depart from me, Spirit of God, for I desire only to live in You.*

HEN Paul had laid his hands on them, the Holy Spirit came upon them, and they spoke in tongues and prophesied. —Acts 19:6

NOV. 7

REFLECTION. When we live in the Holy Spirit, then even our different languages and the variety of how we see things no longer divide us.

We begin to see these differences as a richness for it reminds us that God reveals the truth to us in so many ways.

PRAYER. *Speak to me, Spirit of God, in and through the many different forms of expression that I encounter each day.*

FOR the desires of the flesh are opposed to the Spirit, and those of the Spirit are opposed to the flesh. —Gal 5:17

NOV. 8

REFLECTION. The desire for pleasure can easily lead us off course. The material world, in itself, is good for God created it to be good. Yet, because of sin, it is so easy to misuse it.

This is why we must use the things of this world carefully.

PRAYER. *Give me perspective, Holy Spirit, so that I may use the good things of this world for the good.*

MY message and my proclamation were not made with persuasive words of wisdom, but in a demonstration of the Spirit and of power. —1 Cor 2:4

NOV. 9

REFLECTION. Paul had tried to preach with earthly wisdom when he spoke with the philosophers in Athens. That failed, so he resolved to preach only with a heavenly wisdom, the wisdom of the Cross.

While this wisdom makes no sense in earthly terms, it does in spiritual terms.

PRAYER. *May I embrace the wisdom of the Cross, Spirit of God, and live its mystery with joy.*

OU spare all things because they belong to You, O Lord and lover of souls, for Your imperishable Spirit is to be found in all things. —Wis 11:26—12:1

NOV. 10

REFLECTION. God breathed His Spirit into us when He created the first human being. There is a bit of God's Spirit within each of our hearts. Thus, God sees something of Himself when He looks at each one of us.

We are called to see ourselves and others as God sees us.

PRAYER. *May I always remember, Lord, that I am created in Your image and likeness.*

AKE the helmet of salvation, the sword of the Spirit, which is the Word of God. —Eph 6:17

NOV. 11

REFLECTION. When he was younger, St. Martin of Tours dedicated himself to military service. When he heard the call of Christ, he realized that his call was to fight a spiritual battle. His armor and weapons were virtue and a life guided by the Spirit of God.

Do I consider my spiritual life to be a type of battle against the forces of evil?

PRAYER. *Arm me with the armor of virtue, Spirit of God, Your weapons of faith, hope, and charity.*

HEN Balaam raised up his eyes and saw the Israelites encamped . . . the Spirit of the Lord came upon him . . . —Num 24:2

NOV. 12

REFLECTION. Balaam had been invited by the Moabites to curse Israel. The Holy Spirit came upon him and impelled him to bless Israel and to curse Moab.

The Holy Spirit would not allow Balaam to lie for the Holy Spirit is a Spirit of truth.

PRAYER. *Guide me, Spirit of Prophets, in Your truth and keep my heart from error.*

OR I know that through your prayers and with the help of the Spirit of Jesus Christ this will result in deliverance for me. —Phil 1:19

NOV. 13

REFLECTION. Even though St. Paul was in prison, he trusted that the prayers of the Philippians and the action of the Holy Spirit would be effective and powerful.

This doesn't necessarily mean that he would be set free. Yet, even if he died, he would die in the Lord.

PRAYER. *Deliver me, Spirit of God, from that which would harm me.*

OU are a letter from Christ entrusted to our care, a letter written not with ink but with the Spirit of the living God . . . —2 Cor 3:3

NOV. 14

REFLECTION. Written documents are external. They might not reflect what is really going on inside of us.

Things written on our hearts are those things which we have internalized. They reflect what we think and believe and choose to live each day of our lives.

PRAYER. *Inscribe Your truth deep in my heart, O Spirit of the Living God.*

N wisdom, there is an *intelligent* spirit that is holy and unique . . . —Wis 7:22

NOV. 15

REFLECTION. Intelligence is often considered to be more of a genetically determined trait than a spiritual gift. Yet, God often works through natural circumstances to effect change.

Could God not also work through genes and chromosomes to shower us with gifts and predispositions toward the good?

PRAYER. *Spirit of God, help me to recognize the ways You work through our natural world to bring about Your will.*

PRAY that the God of our Lord Jesus Christ, the Father of glory, may give you a spirit of wisdom and revelation to know Him.

—Eph 1:17

NOV. 16

REFLECTION. It is only in the Spirit that we can know Who God is and what God wants of us.

God gives us His revelation through the Bible, through the Church, through a voice in our hearts that leads us to the truth, and through others who care for us and love us.

PRAYER. *Holy Spirit, enlighten us with Your revelation.*

HIS is the message of the Lord to Zerubbabel: "Not by an army nor might, but by My Spirit, says the Lord of hosts."

—Zec 4:6

NOV. 17

REFLECTION. Israel would not be renewed by force. It was only by the Spirit of God that the people of Israel would be made into who God wanted them to be: a holy people consecrated to God.

This is still true today. Love is stronger than power or force.

PRAYER. *Fortify my heart, Author of all good, and consecrate me to Your will.*

THIS is the reason why the Gospel was preached even to the dead, so that . . . they might enjoy the life of God in the Spirit. —1 Pet 4:6

NOV. 18

REFLECTION. When Jesus died on the Cross, He descended into the underworld (sometimes called Hades or Hell) where He invited people to live in the glory of God in heaven. These were the people who had not heard His message but who had lived good lives.

He did not force them to go to heaven; He only invited them.

PRAYER. *I pray for the poor souls in Purgatory, O Lord, and especially for my loved ones.*

REPENT and be baptized every one of you . . . and you will receive the gift of the Holy Spirit. —Acts 2:38

NOV. 19

REFLECTION. From the first day of the Church, Pentecost Sunday, we have been called to turn away from sin and embrace the gift of the Holy Spirit.

This is done at our Baptism, but it is also done over and over again every time we embrace the Good News.

PRAYER. *I renew my commitment to You, God, and promise You my life and my love.*

OHN also gave this testimony, saying, "I saw the Spirit descending from heaven like a dove, and it came to rest on Him."

—Jn 1:32

NOV. 20

REFLECTION. The Holy Spirit appears in the form of a dove because the dove in the Old Testament is the symbol of love.

In this Gospel, the Spirit remains upon Jesus because God would never abandon Him, just as He would never abandon His Church until the end of time.

PRAYER. *Gracious Dove, Spirit of God, remain with us always.*

N wisdom there is a spirit that is *unstained* and certain . . .

—Wis 7:22

NOV. 21

REFLECTION. The Spirit of God is pure and holy and kept Mary from the damage caused by sin and selfishness. We call this privilege the dogma of the Immaculate Conception.

That same Spirit of purity calls us to turn our hearts over to the Lord so that we may be made pure as well.

PRAYER. *Immaculate Virgin Mary, pray for us.*

E filled with the Spirit, as you sing psalms and hymns and spiritual songs with one another. **—Eph 5:18-19**

NOV. 22

REFLECTION. Many Catholics have an aversion to singing in the liturgy. Yet, when we want to celebrate, we often sing out loud, e.g., patriotic songs, Happy Birthday, golden oldies, etc.

If we are filled with God's Spirit of joy and celebration, we will raise up our voices in Church as well.

PRAYER. *Sing to the Lord; praise His name.*

AKE every possible effort to preserve the unity of the Spirit through the bond of peace. **—Eph 4:3**

NOV. 23

REFLECTION. St. Clement, one of the first popes, wrote to the Corinthian community which was experiencing a period of strife and division. He encouraged them to forgive and accept each other.

It is the Spirit Who gives us the ability to live in true peace.

PRAYER. *Spirit of Peace, calm the discord in our world, and especially in my family and my own heart.*

ITH the help of the Holy Spirit Who dwells in us, guard the treasure that has been entrusted to us.

—2 Tim 1:14

NOV. 24

REFLECTION. We have been taught about our faith in the instructions we received as children, in our study of Catholic teaching, in our prayer and reflection upon the Word of God, etc. We are called to hold on to this treasure and reject false ideas that would endanger our faith.

The Holy Spirit gives us the courage and wisdom to embrace and preserve that truth.

PRAYER. *O Holy Spirit, I cannot even begin to thank You enough for the gift of my faith.*

HE Spirit of Truth Whom the world cannot accept because it neither sees Him nor knows Him . . .

—Jn 14:17

NOV. 25

REFLECTION. The truth of the Good News is something that the world simply cannot understand. It makes no sense if one tries to grasp it logically.

If, on the other hand, one is willing to embrace the Gospel contradictions that one has to die to live in Christ, that love destroys hate, that we have to surrender to conquer, etc., then one will understand the logic of the Cross.

PRAYER. *Teach me the truth of Your Cross, O Spirit of God, and give me the courage to embrace that wisdom.*

VERYONE who speaks a word against the Son of Man will be forgiven, but the person who blasphemes against the Holy Spirit will not be forgiven. —Lk 12:10

NOV. 26

REFLECTION. It is through the action of the Holy Spirit that our sins are forgiven.

The sin against the Holy Spirit is to believe our sins are greater than God's mercy (thus keeping us from accepting God's mercy) or presuming upon God's mercy (not seeking true forgiveness but only playing a game).

PRAYER. *I am a sinner, O Holy Spirit; shower Your mercy and pardon upon me.*

FTER three and a half days, the breath of life from God entered them [the two witnesses]. —Rev 11:11

NOV. 27

REFLECTION. Jesus was raised after three days, so also those who die with Jesus would rise on the third day.

But here we see three and one-half days, for the persecution at the end of time would last three and one-half periods of time. While the persecution lasted for years, the time until their vindication would only be days.

PRAYER. *Come quickly, O Life-giving Spirit, and vindicate my cause with Your love.*

OR it is through the Spirit and by faith that we eagerly hope to attain righteousness. —Gal 5:5

NOV. 28

REFLECTION. One of the hopes of a God-filled life is that our love will continue to grow and grow until it reaches its fulfillment in heaven. It is the Spirit Who tells us that this hope is not futile.

God promises that He will always be faithful to us. The gift of the Spirit, in fact, is the down payment on that promise.

PRAYER. *Gift of God, fill my heart with Your hope and trust.*

WILL not blot out his name [the person who is victorious] from the book of life. —Rev 3:5b

NOV. 29

REFLECTION. Our names were written in the book of life before the foundation of the world. God brought us into being so that we might share in His life and love forever.

Only sin can blot our names out of that book for sin is a rejection of what God called us to be.

PRAYER. *May I never do anything that would blot my name out of the book of life.*

E are witnesses to these things, as is the Holy Spirit Whom God has given to those who obey Him. —Acts 5:32

NOV. 30

REFLECTION. The Holy Spirit gives witness to the truths of our faith both by speaking in our hearts to reveal and confirm those truths and by giving us the courage to be willing to share those truths with others.

Do I have the courage to speak openly of my faith?

PRAYER. *Give me the courage, O Spirit of Truth, to give witness to the Good News each day of my life.*

HE natural person refuses to accept what pertains to the Spirit of God, for to him such things are foolish. —1 Cor 2:14

DEC. 1

REFLECTION. If we choose to adopt an earthly logic, then it will lead us to conclusions that are not always consistent with our faith. The world tells us to look out for number one, to seek revenge on those who have hurt us, to try to get ahead even if that means that we have to push others out of the way.

These are not the ways of the Spirit.

PRAYER. *Let all my thoughts and my goals be consistent with Your logic, O Spirit of God.*

AS he listened to the report, the Spirit of God rushed upon him and he became enraged.

—1 Sam 11:6

DEC. 2

REFLECTION. King Saul heard about the sufferings of his countrymen and he was filled with a righteous spirit of rage.

The Spirit often uses things that happen in our lives to trigger a strong response (e.g., anger, disgust) so that we might fight for justice for ourselves and especially for those who can't defend themselves.

PRAYER. *Spirit of God, may I recognize Your voice that at times speaks through my feelings and emotions.*

GO, therefore, and make disciples of all nations, baptizing them in the name of the Father, and of the Son, and of the Holy Spirit. **—Mt 28:19**

DEC. 3

REFLECTION. The Holy Spirit invites us, like St. Francis Xavier, to share our faith with others. This faith, a gift of the Spirit, is the most precious thing we could ever give to another.

Am I willing to share my faith, especially with those who are seeking meaning in their lives?

PRAYER. *Holy Spirit, give me the courage to share my faith in word and deed.*

DO you not know that your body is the temple of the Holy Spirit within you . . . and that you are not your own.

—1 Cor 6:19

DEC. 4

REFLECTION. God did not create us to be self-centered and selfish. He created us to live a life of dignity.

The Holy Spirit dwells in our hearts. Our bodies are thus the temple that houses the presence of God.

PRAYER. *May I treat my body with the respect due it, caring for the gift that God has given me.*

IN wisdom there is a spirit that is all powerful and all-seeing . . .

—Wis 7:23

DEC. 5

REFLECTION. We live in a world in which things, at times, seem to be out of control. The disasters that we face upon the earth seem to be guided by the forces of evil.

It is an act of faith to believe with our whole heart that God is both all powerful and also that He is able to make good come from those disasters.

PRAYER. *I do believe, O Spirit of Wisdom, that You guide all the events of my life.*

HE fruit of the Spirit is . . . *kindness*, generosity, faithfulness, gentleness and self-control. —Gal 5:22-23

DEC. 6

REFLECTION. The tradition of St. Nicholas and how that tradition evolved into the figure of Santa Claus reminds us that we are called to share those treasures that God has given us (whether they be treasures that are financial, or of time, or of talent).

The more we have been given, the more we are called to share with those who have less.

PRAYER. *As I prepare for Christmas, O Lord, fill me with Your Spirit of kindness and generosity.*

AY my prayer be like incense before You, the lifting up of my hands like the evening sacrifice. —Ps 141:2

DEC. 7

REFLECTION. Incense is said to be a symbol of how our prayers rise up into the heavens where the Holy Spirit presents them to the Father.

But prayer is not just a mist or smoke that quickly disperses. It also powerfully changes reality, for the Spirit uses these God-filled words to transform this world into God's kingdom.

PRAYER. *May my every breath, O Spirit of God, be a prayer that rises up to the heavens.*

OU have probed my heart and examined me throughout the night. You have tested me and found no malice in me. —Ps 17:3

DEC. 8

REFLECTION. The Holy Spirit showered the Blessed Virgin with love from the moment of her conception so that she never felt the damage of the first sin nor did she ever sin herself.

We ask her assistance in purifying our hearts and lives so that we might have her freedom and love.

PRAYER. *Immaculate Virgin Mary, pray for us.*

F it is pleasing to God Almighty, he will be filled with a spirit of understanding. —Sir 39:6

DEC. 9

REFLECTION. We can learn many things and even give our assent of faith, but it does not always mean that we understand these things.

There are graced moments when the Spirit gives us that gift. If even for just a moment, we catch an insight into things that before were confusing and mysterious to us.

PRAYER. *Help me to understand, Holy Spirit, Who You are and what You want of me.*

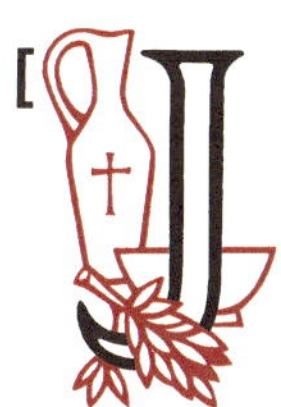

[JOHN the Baptist said], "The One on Whom you see the Spirit descend and rest is the One Who is to baptize with the Holy Spirit." —Jn 1:33

DEC. 10

REFLECTION. The Prophets of the Old Testament and John the Baptist, the precursor of the Messiah, all preached conversion. But Jesus calls us to much more than conversion from sin. He gives us the gift of the Holy Spirit to make us one with God.

The love of the Spirit fills the most profound void of our hearts.

PRAYER. *Send Your Holy Spirit into my heart once again, Lord, and fill me with Your life.*

THEN Elisha, filled with a double portion of his Spirit, worked many marvels with his word alone. —Sir 48:12

DEC. 11

REFLECTION. Elisha asked for a double portion of Elijah's spirit before Elijah was taken up into the heavens on a fiery chariot. The request was granted, for Elisha was able to perform great miracles.

Asking for the gift of the Spirit is not selfish as long as one intends to use the gift for the good of others and the glory of God.

PRAYER. *Grant me, Spirit of God, the gift that I most need, the gift of . . . .*

HERE can I go to hide from Your Spirit? Where can I flee from Your presence? —Ps 139:7

DEC. 12

REFLECTION. There are times that we hope God is not looking because we are embarrassed by what we have done. This is why Adam and Eve hid themselves when they sinned.

But there was no running away from God's Spirit, for the Spirit knows us better than we know ourselves.

PRAYER. *May I never do anything, Lord, that I would not want You to see.*

OW this Lord is the Spirit, and where the Spirit of the Lord is, there is freedom. —2 Cor 3:17

DEC. 13

REFLECTION. What does it mean to be free? It does not mean that we can do whatever we want to do. That would be to enslave ourselves to our passions.

True freedom is to live in the love of the Holy Spirit who calls us to generosity and availability. The Holy Spirit teaches us the true meaning of love.

PRAYER. *Guide me into Your freedom, O Spirit of God, and preserve me from sin.*

O not neglect the gift that was bestowed upon you when, as a result of prophecy, the elders laid their hands on you. —1 Tim 4:14

DEC. 14

REFLECTION. Even in the early days of the Church, the Apostles passed on their authority through a laying on of hands. The Holy Spirit acts through the sacraments to continue the action of Christ upon the earth.

It is good to reflect upon each of the sacraments and ask ourselves what they tell us about Christ and the Church.

PRAYER. *Spirit of God, ever near, help me to experience Your presence and action through the sacraments.*

HE one who searches hearts knows the mind of the Spirit, because the Spirit intercedes for the saints in accordance with God's will.—Rom 8:27

DEC. 15

REFLECTION. It is good to know that someone is always standing in our corner. The Holy Spirit intercedes for us, lifting up our needs and prayers to the Father.

The Spirit desires what is good for us, even when we don't know enough to want what is good for ourselves.

PRAYER. *Spirit of God, intercede for me to the Father.*

THE Spirit of God made me; the breath of the Almighty enlivens me.

—Job 33:4

DEC. 16

REFLECTION. We sometimes think of creation as something that happened long ago, and now the world just continues on its own. Job reminds us that God sustains us in being.

Every second is a gift from God, every flower a continuation of the miracle of God's creative love.

PRAYER. *Open my eyes, O Creating Spirit of God, to the wonders unfolding before my eyes.*

HE had seven horns and seven eyes, which are the seven spirits of God sent forth into the entire world.

—Rev 5:6

DEC. 17

REFLECTION. In Apocalyptic literature, horns stand for authority. Seven is the perfect number, so Jesus possesses all of God's authority.

Eyes stand for the possession of the gifts of the Spirit. Seven eyes mean that Jesus is overflowing with these gifts.

PRAYER. *Jesus, You possess all authority in heaven and on earth. Shower Your gift of the Spirit upon me and the Church.*

WISH you to understand that no one speaking under the influence of the Spirit of God says, "May Jesus be cursed."

—1 Cor 12:3

DEC. 18

REFLECTION. Some in the Corinthian community wanted to reject Jesus because they felt that His material body made Him inferior to totally spiritual beings. They even cursed Him, claiming they were speaking through the Holy Spirit.

St. Paul tells the community that the Spirit leads us to worship Jesus for He is both God and man.

PRAYER. *Blessed be Jesus, Who is both God and man, existing from all eternity and born in a stable.*

ISDOM, who is one, can do anything and renews everything.

—Wis 7:27a

DEC. 19

REFLECTION. We can become frustrated in our spiritual life because we just don't seem to be able to make as much progress as we would have wished.

Yet, by turning our hearts over to the Spirit, we can be renewed. We cannot do it on our own, but with God's grace, anything is possible.

PRAYER. *Fill me, Holy Spirit, with Your grace so that I may be obedient to Your will.*

F there is any consolation in Christ, any comfort in love, any fellowship in the Spirit . . . make my joy complete by being of the same mind . . . **—Phil 2:1-2**

DEC. 20

REFLECTION. The greatest joy that St. Paul could have was to hear that those he knew and loved in Philippi were living an exemplary Christian life.

It was not a question of selfish pride. It was a holy satisfaction in the fact that the Kingdom had dawned in their hearts.

PRAYER. *As we approach Christmas, may my family be an example of Spirit-filled peace.*

E shines as a light for the upright in the darkness; kindness, mercy, and justice are His hallmarks. **—Ps 112:4**

DEC. 21

REFLECTION. As we approach the shortest day of the year, we can reflect on how much we need the light of the world whose birth we celebrate in only a few days.

It is in light of Him that we understand the true meaning of the words kindness, mercy and even justice.

PRAYER. *Holy Spirit, open my eyes to see Christ's light and my heart to be filled with His virtues.*

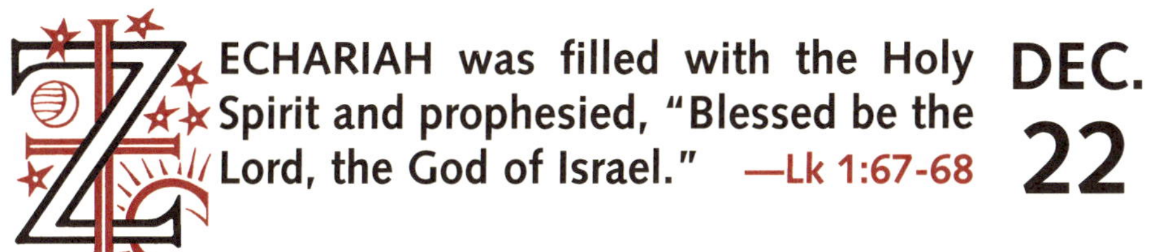

ZECHARIAH was filled with the Holy Spirit and prophesied, "Blessed be the Lord, the God of Israel." —Lk 1:67-68

DEC. 22

REFLECTION. In the light of the Holy Spirit, Zechariah could understand that the birth of his son, John the Baptist, was a sign that God was fulfilling His promises to Israel.

The people around him only saw a normal baby boy; Zechariah saw a miracle of grace. In light of this, there was only one thing he could do: praise the Lord.

PRAYER. *St. John the Baptist, pray for us.*

TEACH me to do Your will, for You are my God. Let Your gracious Spirit lead me along a level path. —Ps 143:10

DEC. 23

REFLECTION. The Psalmist sees his life as a journey whose origin and goal is God. He cannot hope to find his way back home unless he is guided there by God's Spirit.

He prays that the journey not be too arduous (mountains, chasms, etc), lest he lose his way and become discouraged.

PRAYER. *God, widen the road and ease the path that will lead me back to You.*

THE Spirit and the Bride say, "Come!" Let each listener say, "Come!"

—Rev 22:17

DEC. 24

REFLECTION. During Advent, we really await two comings. Obviously, we await the birth of Jesus in Bethlehem, a feast that we celebrate tomorrow.

But we also await Jesus' coming in glory at the end of time. The Holy Spirit reminds us that we are not just living for the present. We must keep our eyes fixed on eternity.

PRAYER. *Give me perspective, Spirit of God, so that I may live for eternity.*

FOR wisdom is an aura of God's might and a pure effusion of the Almighty's glory.

—Wis 7:25

DEC. 25

REFLECTION. The ancients often spoke of light in terms of its purity and power. It was one of the few realities which could give a sense of the glory of God.

The Holy Spirit is both a reflection of the glory of the Father and the Son, and also a source of light to illumine the darkest corners of our soul.

PRAYER. *Holy Spirit of Wisdom, shine Your light of truth and glory upon me.*

TEPHEN, filled with the Holy Spirit, looked up intently to heaven and saw the glory of God and Jesus standing at God's right hand. **—Acts 7:55**

DEC. 26

REFLECTION. Stephen was the first martyr of the Church. The Holy Spirit granted him the courage to give witness to Jesus by his death.

This fulfilled Jesus' promise that we will know what to say when we are on trial for our faith.

PRAYER. *May I always know what to say when I am challenged to give witness to my faith.*

HEN they [Peter and John] arrived there [Samaria], they prayed for them that they might receive the Holy Spirit. **—Acts 8:15**

DEC. 27

REFLECTION. The Jewish people at the time of Jesus hated the Samaritans. They considered them to be heretical Jews. Yet, the Holy Spirit led the Apostles and disciples to Samaria to preach to them.

The Holy Spirit heals the hurts caused by prejudice and judgmentalism.

PRAYER. *Lead me, Spirit of God, to those who most need to hear Your Word.*

JUST as in those days, the child who was born through the flesh persecuted the child who was born through the Spirit.

—Gal 4:29

DEC. 28

REFLECTION. St. Paul refers to the two sons of Abraham as the sons of the flesh (slavery) and of the spirit (freedom). He compares this to the law and faith.

If we live in the freedom of the Spirit, though, it does not mean that all will go well. There is always a cost when we give witness to the truth.

PRAYER. *Give me the courage to live in Your freedom, Lord, and to give witness to Your love.*

IF we live by the Spirit, let us also be guided by the Spirit. We should not become conceited . . .

—Gal 5:25-26

DEC. 29

REFLECTION. The Gifts of the Spirit should not fill us with pride. They were gifts given to us in trust. The Spirit intends us to use them to serve others.

Am I a humble person?

PRAYER. *Let me only boast in You, O Spirit of God, and never treat the gifts You have given me as my own possession.*

HE root of wisdom is fear of the Lord and her branches are found in length of days. —Sir 1:18

DEC. 30

REFLECTION. If we live with the proper attitude of reverential awe toward God, then we will prosper. This doesn't mean that we will become rich or always be happy, but we certainly will be filled with God's joy.

Our days, no matter how long they might be, will be meaningful and blessed.

PRAYER. *May I always stand in awe of Your greatness, Lord, and never cease praising You.*

HILE they were worshiping the Lord and fasting, the Holy Spirit said, "Set Barnabas and Saul apart for me. . . ." —Acts 13:2

DEC. 31

REFLECTION. When we pray and fast, we open up our hearts to the promptings of the Holy Spirit. We can discern the mission that the Spirit has in mind for us.

As we celebrate the end of the year and prepare our New Year's resolutions, we should listen to that Spirit with prayer and fasting.

PRAYER. *May this New Year be a holy year, filled with Your love, O Lord.*

HOLY WEEK

PALM SUNDAY

OD anointed Jesus of Nazareth with the Holy Spirit and power. He went around doing good and healing all . . . —Acts 10:38

REFLECTION. On Palm Sunday, the entire crowd was filled with enthusiasm. Inspired by the Holy Spirit, they recognized who Jesus was: the Son of David.

Yet, it was some of these same people who called for His death days later.

PRAYER. *May my enthusiasm for You, O Lord, never turn into rejection or indifference.*

HOLY THURSDAY

EHOLD, I am standing at the door knocking. If one of you hears My voice and opens the door, I will come in . . . —Rev 3:20

REFLECTION. There are many images that describe the relationship to which God calls us in the Holy Spirit: we are God's children, Christ's brothers and sisters, His friends, His co-workers, etc.

Here we are asked to be His companions (which means to share bread with Him).

PRAYER. *May I always reverence the Holy Eucharist as the body and blood of Christ.*

GOOD FRIDAY

S high priest that year, he was prophesying that Jesus was to die for the nation.

—Jn 11:51

REFLECTION. Those who had chosen an evil path decided to put Jesus to death, and yet God used even their hateful actions to produce a good result. It is through His death that we have acquired salvation.

The Spirit of God can transform every cross into a moment of grace.

PRAYER. *Transform my difficulties and brokenness in Your love, O Spirit of God, so that they might be moments of grace.*

HOLY SATURDAY

HOEVER believes in Me, as scripture has said, "Streams of living water shall flow from within him." **—Jn 7:38**

REFLECTION. The streams of living water about which Jesus is speaking is the life of the Holy Spirit that flows into our hearts.

Just as the breath of God made Adam a living creature, so also the living water of the Holy Spirit gives us abundant life.

PRAYER. *Quench the thirst of my heart, O Life-giving Spirit of God, and renew Your life within me.*

EASTER SUNDAY

O it is with the resurrection of the dead. . . . What is sown is a physical body, what is raised is a spiritual body. —1 Cor 15:42-44

REFLECTION. When Jesus was raised from the dead, He had a glorified body. It was not subject to the limitations of time or space. He would never die again.

What happened to Him on Easter Sunday will happen to each of us who are faithful to His Word.

PRAYER. *Raise me up, O Spirit of God, and give me a never-ending share in Your life.*